Living the Life

Also by David J. Rothman

Poetry
Part of the Darkness
The Book of Catapults
Beauty at Night
The Elephant's Chiropractor
Dominion of Shadow

Editor
The Geography of Hope: Poets of Colorado's Western Slope

Social Science
Hollywood's America: Social and Political Themes
  in Motion Pictures (with Stanley Rothman and Stephen Powers)

More Praise for David J. Rothman's
Living the Life: Tales from America's Mountains & Ski Towns

"Mountains and the sports they inspire are fertile ground for human creativity. In the case of David Rothman, the snowy heights extract words: essays of wisdom, humble experience and awe for the land he carves with the steel edges of his skis. Here, you will find insight into the people of the snow, the land of winter—and a man who chose to live in the midst of it all as a writer, ski racer, mountaineer and father. Share Rothman's experience and come away with a deeper understanding of what calls men to mountains."
— LOUIS DAWSON II, *wildsnow.com*

"It's a select few who let their passion dictate their lifestyle. Doing so requires the sacrifice of a certain sense of normalcy, but the payback is tenfold in experiences that are extraordinary. Rothman is one of those few, and he articulates the highs, and lows, of that life choice perfectly in these pages. *Living the Life* is about one man's relationship with the mountains, but the stories are applicable to anyone who lets his passion lead the way."
— DEREK TAYLOR, EDITOR, *mtnadvisor.com*, EDITOR, *Powder*, 2007-12

"Poet, powderhound, musician, ex-racer, teacher, philosopher–all sides of Renaissance man David Rothman are on display in this collection, which ranges from satire to whimsy to the profoundly grateful and the essential questioning. Emerson? Check. Thoreau? Check. Petrarch? Only David Rothman would put Petrarch in a story about skiing's "earthly enjoyment." In a voice that sparkles with intelligence, he is capable, in the end, of deep sincerity. So spake "The Dude in the Parking Lot," who says of a late-season epiphany at Arapaho Basin: "All that really matters is being there." David Rothman is a writer who skis and a skier who writes, very well."
— PETER SHELTON, AUTHOR OF *Climb to Conquer*
AND *The Snow Skier's Bible*

"David has tuned his words as well as his skis, and this collection offers the equivalent of playful jump turns, graceful arcs and high-speed cruisers. His metaphors made me laugh out loud and look around the coffee shop for someone to read them to. He can be affectionate and smart-ass, funny and philosophical. I felt like I knew these characters (okay, I *do* know some of them) — kids and reprobates, mountaineers and academics. At times David's words conjured the wind-nip on my cheeks, snow billowing over my skis or a warm campfire surrounded by friends, and I thought, 'Wow, he nailed it.'"

—SANDY FAILS, EDITOR, *Crested Butte Magazine*

"If you're supposed to write what you know about, Rothman is clearly in his element on skis in the mountains. This is a mesmerizing compilation of essays as deep as the Wasatch snowpack."

—EUGENE BUCHANAN, EDITOR/PUBLISHER, *Paddling Life*, AUTHOR OF *Brothers on the Bashkaus* AND *Outdoor Parents, Outdoor Kids*

"Through a series of poignant and powerful personal essays, David Rothman exposes a soul skier's raison d'etre. Anyone who rides, glides, or slides on snow will appreciate the mountain tales told in *Living the Life*."

—LANCE WARING

"Riders of the snow who still appreciate words will enjoy *Living the Life*. Rothman's tales, poetic in bursts, transcend the experience of skiing and connect it to the paths we stride, glide and stumble through in everyday life. It is Rothman's take on how skiing is life, how it is not just the path, but also the mountain the path climbs."

—CRAIG DOSTIE, FOUNDING PUBLISHER AND EDITOR, *Couloir*

"Sometimes, while skiing with my wife, I ask her, 'Why is this so much fun?' I ask it in part because no ski writer has managed to answer that question. Radically different from any ski writing I've read are these essays by David Rothman, who gives us the big picture. His enthusiasm for skiing and skiers, for mountains and snow, is infectious. He takes us behind the scenes, into his head and ours, for a look at what skiing really is—a way of life."

—WYN COOPER, AUTHOR OF *Chaos is the New Calm*

Living the Life

Tales from America's Mountains & Ski Towns

DAVID J. ROTHMAN

A Division of Samizdat Publishing Group

CONUNDRUM PRESS A Division of Samizdat Publishing Group.
PO Box 1279, Golden, Colorado 80402

A Division of Samizdat Publishing Group, LLC.

Living the Life: Tales from America's Mountains & Ski Towns.

For information, email info@conundrum-press.com.

ISBN: 978-1-938633-32-4

Front cover photo: Chuck Feil
Back cover photo: David J. Rothman
Author photo: Ernest Hilbert

Library of Congress Cataloging-in-Publication Data is available upon request.

Conundrum Press books may be purchased with bulk discounts for educational, business, or sales promotional use. For information please email: Conundrum Press online: conundrum-press.com

Acknowledgments

I am grateful to the editors of the following journals for permission to reprint material that first appeared with them, sometimes in different form:

cold drill: "God's Lost Tomatoes"
Couloir: "Going Solo," "Tonic of Taconic," "The Year of the Thunderbolt"
Crested Butte Magazine: "Breaking Trail," "Send in the Clowns," "Nick Rayder, Mountain Town Clown," "Sartorial Styles of the Butte," "The Kids Are Alright," "Back to the Butte," "Baptism by Single Track"
Gunnison Valley Journal: "Sweet"
Off-Piste: "The Chute"
Powder: "Dream Line," "The Off-Season," "Big Saturday in the Wawayandas," "Kasha Rigby: A Creative Way To Live"
Ski Racing Online: "To an Athlete Dying Young"
Snow Country: "Carving the Big One"
Telemark Skier: "Making Sure it Goes On," "Bridget Goes to Monarch."
Telluride Magazine: "Sixteen Turns"
Vertical: "Grease"

Many friends and editors improved these essays along the way. I particularly want to thank Steve Casimiro, Lou Dawson, Craig Dostie, Sandy Fails, Derek Taylor, Lance Waring, and Lise Waring for their support and skill. I also owe a great debt to my editors at Conundrum, Sonya Unrein and Caleb Seeling, for supporting this project. As always, my greatest debt is to my family, my boys Jacob and Noah, who inspire me, and my wife, Emily, who puts up with an awful lot of dirt in the car.

In loving memory of Asher Crank and Colin Weston,
Who gave far more to me than I gave to them;
And for my own boys, Jacob and Noah,
Who I hope will find their own paths
To living the life.

Contents

Part Two

Making Sure It Goes On

Part Three

Living the Life

Introduction

The Name of the Place

"Skiing is not a sport, it is a way of life."—Otto Schniebs

My old friend Brooke taught English at the University of Utah for many decades. He was a courageous man, an existential hero, though such blunt praise might have made him uncomfortable. When I was earning my Master's degree in English in the early 1980s, I got to know Brooke in part through backcountry ski touring, and although he was a gifted teacher, I came to like him far too much ever to want to take a class from him. I didn't want to put him in the situation of him having to give me a grade—I wanted to hang out together and enjoy life, which we did. There was the blues guitar playing he loved, long meals and conversations, rambunctious dancing. I remember one night jumping around to Rory Gallagher at the old Zephyr Club in downtown Salt Lake when Brooke practically made the floor shake. We also went on big ski tours in the Wasatch and in other relatively unskied ranges of the state—the Stansbury Mountains, the Uintas.

Brooke's wife Peggy taught philosophy. I played the piano at their wedding reception, a long time ago. One time, a few years after I'd left Utah, my wife Emily and I were visiting Brooke and Peggy in their cabin near Capitol Reef. We climbed Mt. Ellen, the highest peak in the Henry Mountains, the last quadrant in the lower forty-eight to be mapped by the U.S. Geological Survey. From the summit we looked out across the desert seven thousand feet below and watched swifts rocketing the ridges. Over a glass of wine back at the cabin that evening, the conversation turned to what each of us would like to see but realized we probably never would. I forget what I said, but remember that Peggy said she'd like to see, just once, the exact moment when cause meets effect. How do we define the instant when bat hits ball? And where did that cause begin? When the pitcher threw? When the batter stepped into the box? When they both decided to play baseball that day? When their parents took them to Little League practice twenty years ago? When the game was invented? You get the idea. A hard thing to figure out.

That conversation has stayed with me. While we may not see it happen, the joining of cause and effect becomes clearer in retrospect, when we can see both parts of it reaching out over time. We can't even hope to describe this process without a decent memory, but since humans have highly developed cortex functions, we have a chance.

* * *

The seeds of this book were planted over seventy years ago, when my mother's mother would not allow her daughter, Eleanor, to go skiing. Twenty years later, when Ellie was thirty and her life was her own, she packed us all into the car and headed north. Now, at seventy-nine, my mother still skis over twenty-five days a year.

My memory of that day at Mt. Snow, Vermont, the first day I ever went skiing, is splashed with blue, the deepest sky blue, bluer than any blue could ever be. Pine trees line the side of the impossibly white hill, which seems immense but is not, as it is the smallest learning pitch tucked in at the bottom of the resort. It's served by a low, slow clanking chair that lumbers uphill like an old coal train. I recall a sensation of warmth. Warmth seeps into the memory itself until it is not only a memory but also a promise, though of what is hard to say.

My father is trying to ski on "shorties," solid wood teaching skis popular back then, and he is smoking a cigar, which I think is weird. And it is winter but the sun is blazing and the snow is getting a bit wet on the bottom flats. I can't stop laughing and go tumbling into a flimsy fence. A strange man who seems to be as old as time comes up to me and asks, "Are you alright?" And I still recall that great word, "Yes!" and my laugh as I stand up and scramble around him to get back on the lift, every cell aching to invite gravity to do that to me again.

As for cause and effect? I distinctly remember thinking, "I'm going to do this for the rest of my life." An unambiguous transcendental action of the will as it chooses the good, the beautiful, the true.

* * *

There were the lessons. First would come what seemed like endless hours of anticipation, lacing leather boots as we sat on the lower steps inside at home, then the meandering drive to the local hill, Mt. Tom. Then, although it seemed impossible, there it was, huge meadows of tilted snow and a curriculum: Wedge, (side step), Stem Christie, (hockey stop), Christie, Parallel, Wedeln. Back and forth the mystery snaked across the pitches. As we rode the chairlifts and T-Bars, we quizzed each other about how to do all this stuff. Everyone had a theory. Our instructors gave us incomprehensible instructions about where to put our hands and stick our butts. It was sort of like math, but more fun, although mistakes hurt more, as if the pencil had exploded, broken your nose, and strewn your gear all over the side of a hill.

One cold, gray day, Elizabeth crossed her tips before us all, slowly body-slammed a slick spot right in front of me, and burst into tears. I found that hard to understand. Of course, it was cold and dark, and it was humiliating to fall in front of friends, and you could have gotten hurt—but you didn't, so what's so bad? After all, we're going to live forever, tomorrow the sun will come out, and learning to fly just takes some practice. I tried to cheer her up.

We were only nine or ten. I can't even remember her last name and I don't know what's happened to her, much less if she still skis. She was cute.

* * *

In those years when the first snows came, we'd trudge off to some neighborhood hill, Hospital Hill, Round Hill, Paradise Pond, dragging skis and shovels, make a few turns and then build our own temple, a holy kicker, a happy mix of physics, geometry, and goofy grace.

It's the same everywhere, in every sport that's still a sport rather than a commodity: smiling kids on a street with a soccer ball, splashing in a pool, playing catch, hucking jumps. People allude to this kind of thing as the purpose of sports all the time—fun and friendship—but rarely does anyone get at the heart of it, the cause and effect. Still, the world understands and aches for it. That's why the Olympics run better than the U.N. We should describe the cause and effect of sport, try to understand it so we have something to say when those same boys and girls put aside their games and turn into different people, have forgotten the good that sports can embody. To paraphrase the great Nordic competitor Bill Koch (who single-handedly invented skate-skiing), if more people skied, the world would be a better place.

And the effect that sport can have on life is why it matters so much that back in the day, while some of us sledded and some played hockey, my friends and I would hike up the hill again and again to our kicker and hurl ourselves into space, wild little question marks plowing into the frozen grass. We had enough cartilage to practice helicopters until we were dizzy, and soon we even began to land them. But no matter what, we'd climb again and again until our jeans were soaked, our wool mittens clumped with ice, the last light had faded from the sky, and then we'd trudge home, a pack of happy dogs filled with the joy that comes from having used every single muscle, whistling, bragging, telling jokes, friends for life, or so we thought.

As adults we should put aside childish things—but are sports really childish? Probably no one should get paid $20 million for playing catch, but all of us should probably play catch or swim or kick a ball or practice helicopters with friends until our jeans start to freeze in the dusk. And everyone should try to remember the good such child-like things can create.

There's more. And all of it is part of the reason—the cause—why I am a skier, someone who looks at mountains with a certain eye, why I study maps and aerial photographs to find August turns in a low snow season. If you've read this far, chances are you know why people do this and might even have some stories of your own, stories that only you can tell because each one is a perfect, invisible diamond where cause meets effect. No one can describe or even see it but you, and it is yours to share with others if you choose. We are a community, as the anthropologist Clifford Geertz suggests, because we understand these stories we tell ourselves about ourselves.

* * *

Here is another one of those stories. Very shortly before this book went to press, on July 31, 2013, Brooke Hopkins passed away, requiring me, with sorrow, to change the tenses in some sentences of this introduction. He was seventy-one and the reason I referred to him as "an existential hero" is that he had been confined to a wheelchair for more than four years, ever since a catastrophic road bike accident in Utah's City Creek Canyon left him a quadriplegic, unable even to breathe without mechanical assistance. Brooke's name may be familiar, as the heart-rending cover story of *The New York Times Sunday Magazine* for July 21, 2013—just ten days before his death—was about Brooke and Peggy. His accident came just months after he had retired. As that story recounts, one irony of what had happened is that Peggy is one of the leading scholars on end-of-life bioethics—and she found herself in a situation in which, at any time, her own husband might ask her to help him to end his life.

One of the most astonishing things about Brooke was that after his accident, and after two years of rehabilitation in a traumatic spine-injury facility that many never leave alive, and despite endless pain and life-threatening infections, Brooke returned home . . . and returned to teaching. Enabled by every life-sustaining and communications technology available, this paralyzed giant (he was at least six-foot-six) taught class after class to eager students who came to his home just to discuss literature. According to his obituary in *The Deseret News*, during this time he taught classes in Thoreau's *Walden*, *The Iliad*, *The Odyssey*, *The Aeneid*, *The Divine Comedy*, *The Canterbury Tales*, Shakespeare's *Sonnets*, *Moby Dick*, and *The Tempest*. Not bad for someone who couldn't even turn a page.

This has everything to do with mountains and skiing, because a good piece of my friendship with Brooke, the place where we too talked about many of those books, played out in the mountains. My ski journal from those years is filled with dates and places that remember him, including this entry about a day on the western-most peak of Utah's Uintas, a remote range to the east of Salt Lake:

Saturday, Feb. 4, 1984: Big tour, 3,500'+ gain, up Swift's Canyon to Hoyt Peak, with Brooke and friends. Snow was soft in places, crusted in others. Beautiful inversion weather, and a great view of the Wasatch, Timpanogos, the Uintas, and into Wyoming as far as the eye, etc. Beginning to get the teles more. Very little open terrain on the trail.

My journal for that year alone records at least four major tours with Brooke.

* * *

Life is so rich. Many years later, in February of 2000, I spent a week with Steve Miller and other friends at Golden Alpine Holidays' Vista Hut (for more on that adventure, see *Chapter 10—A Week in a Hut*). The only way to reach the place is by helicopter from a parking lot near Rogers Pass in central British Columbia. One evening I casually picked up *The Norton Anthology of English Literature* from the ragtag library on a shelf and saw that it was inscribed by Gale Dick, now Professor of Physics Emeritus at Utah. Gale is a violinist and a founder of the Chamber Music Society of Salt Lake City, and also a fierce environmentalist who founded SAVE OUR CANYONS, an organization devoted to preserving the wilderness near Salt Lake from over-development. I met Gale through Brooke on one of our tours in those canyons. Then, on Brooke and Peggy's blog, when I was reading posts for Brooke's "virtual birthday" in 2009, lo and behold, there was a post from Gale talking about how "We skied the Selkirks from a hut we reached by helicopter along with Chauncy and Emily, Kip Wallace and Howie Garber. Sang to a guitar, ate well, wore ourselves out climbing and skiing." And there is a precious picture, with Brooke, the tallest, in the back row wearing a huge smile, Gale to his right. I've stood exactly where that photo was taken.

BROOKE, GALE AND FRIENDS AT THE VISTA HUT, 1993. LEFT TO RIGHT: HOWIE
GARBER, SANDRA CAVALCANTI, GALE DICK, EMILY HALL, BROOKE HOPKINS, KIP
WALLACE, CHAUNCY HALL. PHOTOGRAPHER UNKNOWN.

How—why—would anyone separate all this beautiful living—those
long meals, the books, the dancing, the blues, the love and the
sorrow—from the great mountains where so much of it happened?
And yet that is what often occurs in books about our sport, as if
our romance with the alpine world were not also about our lives
at their core. I do not separate my friendship with Brooke from my
friendship with Brooke in the mountains. It all clamors for admis-
sion, all of it, all at once.

* * *

Thinking about my own romance with the alpine world over the
years has led me to discover one of the places where cause and
effect come together. I may not be able to see this place of fusion
clearly, or all at once, but it does exist and I can certainly sense it.

    This book is my attempt to give that place its name. I wrote it
because I wanted to help give American skiing a written language
as soulful as that of fishing, surfing, mountaineering, sailing, golf,

and other environment sports, a quality it seemed to lack when I was growing up. In those days, most ski writing seemed to be about resorts, gear, race results and technique, all of which is fine but doesn't touch the core of the sport, the irresistably emotional, spiritual, vibrant reasons I and so many others feel compelled to build significant parts of our lives around mountains. Ski writing has changed somewhat now, thanks to lifetimes of commitment by the likes of Lou Dawson, Craig Dostie, Lance Waring, Steve Casimiro, Rob Story, Peter Shelton, Mike Finkel, Bill Kerig, Les Anthony, John Fry, Wayne Sheldrake, Roland Huntford, John Allen and others, along with all the people who have helped to bring journals like *Powder*, *Couloir*, *Backcountry*, *Telemark*, *The Ski Journal*, *Off Piste* and others into the light—but there is so much still to explore.

Like other environment sports, skiing does not create a bounded playing field but rather accepts and transforms the places where we pursue it. These essays are windows into how I've lived significant parts of my own life in those places and in that way, and I offer it up in the hopes that it will resonate with yours. For if skiing is not a sport, but a way of life, it touches far more than mountains and snow—it comes into contact with friendship, love, grief, joy, sorrow, history, politics, ambition, faith, tragedy, comedy, failure, triumph, audacity, remorse, delight, and regret, which is to say: everything that matters. It is those deep emotional realities that are at the heart of life.

And you have no choice but to live that life.

So live it.

—*In memoriam*, Brooke Hopkins, 1942 – 2013

Part One

The Year of the Thunderbolt

1

The Chute

Dick, our coach, led the team very early one late May morning north for hours to Pinkham Notch. Out of the green labyrinth of our little town and valley we sped up into wilderness. Roadside at Joe Dodge, pre-dawn, we strapped old-school clunker packs to our high school backs and humped full racks of alpine gear to Howard Johnson's, thousands of feet above. We claimed a lean-to, dumped the camping gear, then followed the trail beneath the Little Headwall up to the Lunch Rocks and the base of Tuck's.

Nothing had prepared me for it, not my homemade trail map wallpaper, or Stenmark, Theoni, Killy, Saudan, carving my ceiling so I could practice the Platonic carve in delta sleep, not studying the topos, knowing the names of every line—Hillman's, Duchess, Left Gully, Chute, Lip and Headwall, Right Gully—not knowing the Inferno history of Brooks Dodge, Toni Matt, and Dick Durrance. Every time I go back, I remember what it was like to come into that cathedral for the first time, already tired but still looking up—no ropes, no lifts, no rules, no nothing except a thousand crazies, kamikaze inner-tubers, frat boys with kegs, a festival of mountain freaks, sunshine so bright I burned off half my skin, and a vertical wall of snow climbing into the sky. And the turns—all made with friends—every single one earned—were each like falling from winged flight into an ocean, yet breaking the old story's mold, feathers, glue intact, the edges suddenly gaining purchase again in the slushy corn a full ten feet lower each time, saying yes I will, yes, as if you could dance down the side of the Chrysler building or a granite elevator shaft filled with diamonds.

At the end of the day, alone near the top of the Chute, I planted my right pole and soared. And it was no disembodied, stammering voice but my own, telling me, in the mountains, there you feel free. Then to roll that knowledge into sleep beneath stars in the middle of a krummholz forest, the constellations burning brightly, milk of a goddess spilling across friends laughing, boasting, telling lies, fart jokes, Dick, Shep, Steve, Rick, Mike, Karl, and then the dawn comes back for another day—after that, when you hike out, fall back into the world, you cannot help yourself—at night you steal out to the garage and ponder the trusty, rusty wings hanging there in the cool summer darkness, urging you to buckle them on your back again and again and again and aspire to the sky.

2

Skunked

My birthday comes in mid-May and for many years I've celebrated it with a solo descent of an unnamed north-facing gully above town. It's only a 1,200-foot climb, but it's forty degrees most of the way, narrow, choked with trees. Don't know why I always want to do this, but I don't think I need a reason.

I like this gully, but nobody else usually wants to ski it with me. I get out early, park at the edge of town, stroll across the approach and up into the woods on an overgrown mining road, punch straight up the line, enjoy the view, then get down and off to work by ten. Not a bad way to start the day and testify to another year on the planet.

That's how I found myself, last spring, all alone in a full-body grovel halfway up the ridge, hanging on to a rotten pine branch and laughing. We'd had a low year—the basin was at less than fifty percent of average snowpack for May—but I'd done my homework, and I was sure there was snow hiding in my little stash. The night before, the mercury had dropped to only about thirty degrees, but there was frost on the deck. So I figured, Why not? When I told my wife where I was going, she just shook her head. She's used to it.

The approach was warm and dry. Too many flowers for this time of year, closed in the crisp morning air but ready to pop. I couldn't skin any of it. Still, I forged on. The snow patches had the look and consistency of filthy snot, but so what, I thought, I'm in the pines and low. It's all good. It will be frozen higher up. It's my birthday and I'm going skiing.

I came to the base of the line and started climbing fall-line, but the crust still wouldn't support my weight. No problem, I decided, I'll climb in the woods, then swam off to the side of the gully. This is where it started to get interesting. AT boots are great for kicking steps in snow or walking on moderately tilted dirt. I'm here to say that they're not the best for bushwhacking muddy forty-degree hillsides. For every couple of steps I took, I slid or stumbled back or sideways, often narrowly avoiding pungee impalement, and the snow patches made it that much worse, as I'd sink to the knees, or hips—wherever the ground was. The stuff was one of the nastiest snow conditions I've ever seen, one for which we need a new name, a word that evokes dirty, wet, rotten, unconsolidated, previously faceted snow. *Flormp? Jizsprat? Klupft?* Something like that.

That was how I wound up in the full-body uphill grovel in the mud, laughing. For in all my absurd striving, it was at that point, after thirty or so slow minutes, when I realized what a beautiful day it was. Somehow that's what it took to get me there, to realize it. The sky was azure. The temperature was good (a little too warm, but what the heck). A gentle breeze riffled the pines. I could hear the sounds of town below. Birds were singing and a Downy Woodpecker was working his way up a tree not far from me. Here and there were piles of pinecone flakes under a tree, signs of some critter or another at home. None of these elements seemed to be struggling—none cared what I was doing—they were part of a harmony which I had obviously misunderstood. I seemed to be the only one striving and cursing in my muddy, misbegotten quest for the heights. I could add in the occasional squirrel who'd go off up in the canopy about my intrusion and chatter at me until I moved out of his territory.

The great guide Reudi Beglinger likes to say that there are only three kinds of snow: good snow, great snow, and a bad attitude. I slowed down, but I kept climbing.

At the top, over the lip of the ridge, I removed my boots and scraped out the dirt and snow that had packed in against the tongues. A few gulps of water, boots back on, and into the bindings.

And then the miracle: the skiing worked. I punched through and went over the bars only three or four times, dangerous in that terrain, but the chance of sliding was zero since I'd just wind up in a shallow hole of *flormp*. Some turns were even good, just enough crust to hold the edge as I dodged saplings. It was my birthday and I was skiing.

I walked back out to the car through a field littered with purple, fuzzy blue pasque flowers, *Pulsatilla Patens*, opening in the spring sun, revealing their bright yellow bundles of stamens. All that fuzzy stuff keeps them warm, lets them bloom early. Went and had a coffee and a breakfast croissant at Al's.

What a great birthday present to myself—another year alive, another trip down Birthday Gully, another lesson about the good news of the mountains. And I thought: *that was great, that was great skiing*, if only to me. If skunked is a state of mind, I wasn't. As Lance Waring has pointed out, every day's a powder day if you just look at it right. It brought me joy. And I promised myself: Same time, next year.

3

Dream Line

I think there's a rope across it now, that gully dropping off the skier's right of lower Chips. And there probably should be, because
it's stupid. But to try telling that to someone who can pull it off in
a glory of arrogance and testosterone poisoning would be like that
old blowhard telling Hamlet, "This above all, to thine own self be
true, etc." And I don't know what anyone else called that line, but
SfB, i.e., "Shit for Brains," is what we called it, laughing at ourselves
as we'd drop in to one of the three vertical finger entries, committed to free fall, facing the gully's ugly other wall.

The trick is never the jump—it's the landing. This one was tricky
because as you came maching out of fifty near-vertical feet of
narrow straight-lining, you had to deftly set a left edge and vector
just right up the angled ramp slightly downhill from your entry on
the opposing side to avoid both the full-on, fall-line, left-side Scylla
of gully-throat acceleration that would lead like a perfect theorem
to inevitable oblivion blowup, or the right-side, smack-down Cha-
rybdis of that bone-crunching wall. But with such a tiny margin
for error, if you did in fact stick the up-angled exit to opposite slot,
you would then crest out at about forty and get hucked like a scud,
knees into your chest, easily twenty-five feet up and a hundred out

over the open slope beyond it, feeling for a few giddy moments like a small telecommunications satellite.

And if the snow were right and you kept your wits about you, hands forward, riding the apex of your own bright rainbow, you could then extend your right leg and land in the deepest, sweetest crud carve imaginable, sailing away laughing and more unscathed than a blue angel, than a proton blowing down an accelerator, than a ray of starlight, than a lover's other in a long, deep, perfect kiss.

Indeed, like a sailor bound singing across the wine-dark waves for home, you could become an utterly imperfect animal fulfilling a beautiful dream.

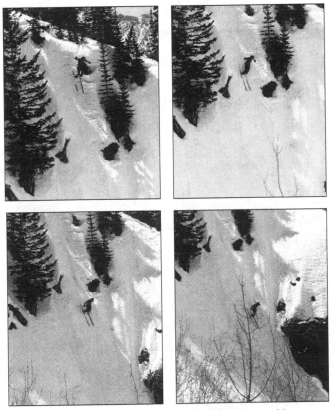

THE AUTHOR DROPS SFB [SHIT FOR BRAINS], SNOWBIRD, APRIL 12, 1986.
PHOTOS BY CHUCK FEIL.

4

Big Saturday in the Wawayandas

I knew something weird, something unprecedented, miraculous and delightful was going on when I turned off Route 23 and headed up into the hills. The day before, I'd watched pictures of houses on the Connecticut coast and Long Island shore kissing their sandy foundations goodbye, and I'd heard reports of a blizzard that was holding court just minutes from the George Washington Bridge. As soon as I could, I headed for my local ski haunt, Hidden Valley, New Jersey, to see if these reports were true, but the splendid facts were almost too much to bear.

I hadn't believed the snow part. I grew up in the east. I've been fooled too many times by predictions of heavy winter based on acorn size and the thickness of squirrel fur, seduced too many times into buying tank after tank of gas by promises of snow softer than the side of the Lincoln Monument, promises almost always broken. Experience has made Eastern skiers more skeptical than Voltaire. But now I was on the approach to Hidden Valley, on December 12, and it looked more like the Selkirks. Fir trees, their boughs bent to the ground under foot after accumulating foot of snow, lined the road like illustrations in a heli-skiing brochure. Abandoned cars were becoming the spines of sculpted drifts. The National Weather Service was telling people not to travel unless it was absolutely necessary. Right. Bring me my chariot of fire.

I've skied deeper and lighter snow, but never on the same day I've also eaten breakfast at Ess-a-Bagel. The long, tall tales are legend—Otis Ridge, a four hundred-foot drop area in the Massachusetts Berkshires, got pasted with over forty inches and the town had to call in the National Guard. Ski Windham, a larger area in the Catskills, reported fifty-two inches of snowfall in under three days. To get to either place from New York on Saturday, you'd have needed a tank, but Hidden Valley, fifty miles from mid-town Manhattan, had received somewhere between two and three feet, more natural snow than they had seen in the last several years combined, and it was within striking distance. I was able to get there in the middle of the worst snowstorm in living memory without having to cancel the rest of my life, and so off I went. I'd be back in New York for dinner at seven—and who knows, maybe the opera.

Hidden Valley is a skier's ski hill. You snake out from the city through the freeway nightmare of Jersey's industrialized marshes and strip developments, eventually leaving the suburbs behind. Soon, smaller roads climb into the hills and follow a few small signs over a pass in the Wawayanda Mountains, then down and around long, steep corners that often cause some of the worst car accidents in the state. Suddenly, there's a hard right onto a side road that climbs abruptly to a small dirt parking lot. Just above the parking lot is the bullwheel and counterweight of a chairlift, and in most years, nothing but lonely tongues of man-made snow on a brown hillside.

The skiing is often good. The management knows how to make snow and the hill is always uncrowded. Twenty thousand vertical feet (a mere thirty-two rides) is no problem most days. It's also steep, genuinely steep, steep enough that one trail is FIS homologated for slalom. The staff runs a first-rate race program, and the mountain has hosted Nor-Am slaloms, pulling them off with panache thanks to hard work and trusty snow cannons. Competitors get a bit of a jolt when they discover how the race hill rolls over and growls about halfway down. It's just that most of the snow doesn't fall from the sky.

Six hundred and forty feet of vertical isn't much, but on that December day, it was the place to be. It was that little hill's turn to stand at the deep heart's core of the ski world. The groomed trails made the skis feel and sound just like they do at Alta, silky and quiet, punctuated by the occasional muffled clicking of one edge against the other. When I hooked up with Bob McGraw, Director of Race Operations, Brian McDermott, Race Coach, and Ken Caffrey, Director of Marketing, the serious fun began. After a short tactical conference, we ducked the rope onto Helen Back, the Nor-Am race trail. There had been little snowmaking before the storm, and the steeper pitches are steep enough. Even so, we didn't bottom out; we bounced down run after run, giving our Gore-Tex a workout in something other than slop, our skis a chance to perform a free-floating flex. Feeling the boards slide and bend in this way within gunshot distance of the Belt Parkway was a bit surreal, but we were ready. We hooted. We hollered. We threw ourselves blithely off the rollers and when we landed, it didn't hurt anywhere. At the bottom of each run, the grins, high-fives, and then the quiet, gentle run-out back to the lift in a single track reminded me of Grand Targhee in a storm, or some small corner of it.

Yes, a few ambitious branches and brambles poked up, and the snow guns on their positioning pulleys above the trail reminded us of where we were. Yes, we knew it couldn't last. When the rains came a few days later, I greeted them with genial denial, sagely lying to myself that it was good for the snowpack, would help it consolidate. Otherwise, I would have cried. Yes, the hill was small and the snow was thicker than it usually is in the Wasatch. But on that day at Hidden Valley, you could feel the spirit of the sport as much as any place, ever. The unbridled happiness of skiers charging through deep, fresh snow in a storm, transforming a winter hillside into dynamic camaraderie, can be as powerful on a short, steep, pitch in New Jersey as in the Alps.

At the end of the day, Bob and I were standing by the race training center. He pointed up to a new timing hut at the bottom of the trail and said "I built that." He paused, then added, "When you write your piece, let them know that even though this is New Jersey, there are mountain people out here too. We ski just about as hard as anyone." As he turned toward the training center, I headed back for one more, down through that excellent weather that can turn even a hill just beyond suburbia into a fragment of bliss.

5

Emigration Canyon
Telemark Baptism

It was Wyn who dragged me up there with promises about a new way to glide the planet, to become more like Antaeus, never leaving it, heels free, locked on only at the toe, which would allow the ball of the foot to flex, follow anatomical structure more truly. That's all you really need to make a turn, two skis lined out into one long edge. It was 1982. Wyn and I were teaching assistants in the English Department at the University of Utah. Telly gear was still spindly stuff, the full setup resembling slippers that had been strapped onto barrel staves. But the people who talked about it—their eyes would widen with secret knowledge, the mysteries of snowpack theirs. They were a true Weather Underground, lecturing from the pit on depth hoar, dendrites, wind slab, sun crust, temperature gradients, the freedom of the hills.

The place Wyn took me was just a small pitch near the road, maybe five hundred vertical feet at most, and I began to learn from him how to apply and rip skins, how to climb, how to turn uphill in a track, how a beacon works and how to find it when it's buried in the snow, how to sift snow in my hands and think about it for myself, how important it is to wear the right clothing, because cotton kills.

I remember the sky gray, friends yelling, spectacular slo-mo crashes, falling like children, playing, holding my hands too high as I tried to re-engineer counter-rotation to fit with the new free-heel placement of feet: the opposite of the Cristiana turn, inside foot back, not forward, weight distribution fifty-fifty. What a concept. I failed miserably, over and over, launching face-first into the slightly crusted mank, laughing like a six-year-old. Then I'd put the skins back on and climb to the top of the pitch, learning the angled platforms of uphill friction.

All of this was long before Wyn, a waiter at the Cliff over at Snowbird, became famous for writing a poem about Bill, the most unlikely muse in the history of art, whom I myself used to hear utter the winning words "All I want to do is have a little fun before I die," and then watch in disbelief as he took another sip of Jack Daniels from a sixteen-ounce cup he held in one hand as he drove the enormous rusting white Ambassador with the other, or fired up some demented needle-born concoction. When I look back, frankly, it's amazing any of us survived, for example, the time on my twenty-fourth birthday when we got profoundly drunk and then when Bill learned I'd never been to a brothel he roared with indignation, threw me in his car, and beelined for the Sultan's Palace, where in the dark parking lot he tossed me over his shoulder, not too difficult for him because he is about six-four, stumbled through the front door and poured me onto the carpet in front of a small crowd of bemused whores, yelling "Screw this guy!" and throwing hundred-dollar bills in the air like candy at the Fourth of July parade.

Or the time at a party somewhere in the Avenues, swill as deep as our ankles—no kidding, they drink hard in that town—Bill for some reason wearing a dress, when I jumped out of a second story

window to prove something and landed in a bush, though I did hook
the gutter on the way down and ripped it off the building, tearing
a huge hole in my pants but emerging unscathed.

Or the time we rocketed over to Wendover on a whim to gamble
all night and the dealer, when we asked her where she was from,
replied "Around," and kept on dealing. Then the Ambassador died
on the way back across the dawn-streaked salt flats and we had to
hitch back to Nevada and ride the Greyhound home.

Or the time Bill, aka Fat Man, the Wump, the Orb, Dr. Wumpen-
houser, went on a two-week tear and for some reason had a
goddamn big car he'd rented in Texas, and Ellen, his long-suffer-
ing girlfriend, asked me to drive it back to Dallas for him because he
just couldn't and so there I was, somewhere between Rawlins and
Laramie, looking up at the coldest, clearest stars while a ground
blizzard completely obscured the highway. The wind eventually
blew the trunk of the car open and started pushing it down the
road using that lifted piece of metal like a sail as I passed jackknifed
semis that reminded me of expired dinosaurs. And I remember
thinking to myself the obvious things, such as "Bill, you're a jerk,"
and "This is ridiculous," and "Well, at least we're saving money on
gas," and "I hope I don't die."

Or the time we went skiing and Ellen, whom Bill called *Chuckles*
and who was a lovely librarian, froze with fear on an intermedi-
ate trail and he lay down on the snow and reached into his jacket
pocket, pulled out a fistful of minis and started tossing them
up the hill, saying, "Rattie, give these to Chuckles. She needs
some encouragement."

Oh, if only all the mothers of America knew what their children
were saying when they sang Wyn's lyric, which became a famous
song about Bill by Cheryl Crow (yes, that song), they would tremble with fear and loathing. Although, while he could get paranoid,
I never saw Bill hurt a fly, in fact he was a good teacher and quite

kind. When I had mono, which I think I probably caught on that cold Nevada morning when we abandoned the Ambassador in the Salt Flats, Bill was the one who came to my apartment and climbed the fire escape with Chinese soup and ice cream, the only things I could eat because my tonsils were the size of golf balls.

And of course all this is just the narratological tip of a tropical storm, one pale streamer of cloud, the living body of it still out there churning across some dark quadrant of a lost Pacific, for I haven't even told you about Gail and Chuck and Brooke and Peggy and AnneMarie—the beautiful AnneMarie—and Barry and Buck and Richard and Liza and Colleen and Penny and Stuart and Kathy and Karen and Gail and Rick her husband, a sweet man as far as I could tell, who ate cyanide in his lab, and so, so many others . . .

But while we're on the subject I will tell you that Bill once owned a construction company called Mammoth Erection, and that he claimed he used to take acid and lie in the grass at the runway terminus as 747s took off.

Bill also had a thirteen-year-old son, Chopper, whom I tutored. During the first session when I came into his basement bedroom, there, on his eighth-grade ceiling, was the Pet of the Month wearing nothing but a dog collar. And one time Bill, who was then living up in Park City, went shopping for lawn furniture with Chopper and couldn't fit it in the car because he'd seen a bunch of helium-inflated balloons he decided to buy as well and with which he had filled the car, so he asked Chopper to lie down on top of the lawn furniture on the roof of the car as he drove slowly home, which of course led to a local policeman pulling him over. I wish I could have been there to see the look on that trooper's face as Bill got out of a car with a fifteen-year-old boy lying prone on folded lawn furniture on top, and all the balloons escaping up and away as he sauntered over to the patrol car, knowing he was busted anyways, so what the hell, he brought his drink, smiling, and by all reports said, "Hi officer, what seems to be the problem?"

And then there was Bill's fairly successful novel, Prisoners, which Larry, whom Bill called Cat Man, once characterized as an extended meditation on cocaine, blowjobs, and hookers. Ah, poor dead Cat Man, he was one of the best poets of his generation, but he beat the crap out of madness in that gentle but intense, interior, utterly cool way he had, I think of him as a gentle ghost. I love that one about the man talking to the horse.

And Larry became a pretty good skier too. We would go up the canyon occasionally and I'd give him a lesson and we had some laughs, and there were fascinating romantic confusions among the various beautiful women whom Wyn and Kurt and Larry and I loved and who graciously made love to us more or less seriatim, each of whom deserves many poems at least partly in recompense for our confused, which is not to say shoddy, behavior, but go ahead, say shoddy.

And I haven't even told you about sitting one night in a little jazz club somewhere downtown when Joe Pass agreed to chat after a show, just a handful of eager young musicians and him graciously showing how he effortlessly played melody, bass, and chords all improvised and rigorous to a fault like a simultaneous backwards Chinese puzzle, eyes a little heavy, sweet virtuoso, sadness, joy and sprezzatura tied to the generosity of that hour in Salt Lake.

Yet all of this connects back to those floppy telemark skis, because as all of this happened, that was something running through it all like an inaudible undertone. I was learning how to ski with a free heel, one climb and one turn after another up and down Little Cottonwood's White Pine, Maybird, Flagstaff, Big's Silver Fork, Mineral Fork. One day in Mineral Fork, now proficient, after climbing hard and long, Jim and I mooned Wasatch Powderbirds as those lazy tourists buzzed us on a sweet ridgetop we'd earned with sweat. We then dropped in northeast, deep fluff all the way, and I got it, I got it, I was making telemark turns through deep drifts of soft diamonds. It was like learning how to walk for the first time, but we were running down the February meadows of a wilderness paradise, our genuflecting knees and hips ergonomically riding that silent white wave in alpine sunshine, the mass of Superior hulking above us at the end of the drainage.

And guess what? Bill's still alive, sixty now, beat his hepatitis, more or less sober, living somewhere in northern California, irresponsible bastard. I still love him. And when I look back on it, contemplating how complicated life is, and how evanescent raw joy and friendship, and how the world tries to stomp it out, and how eventually of course it will succeed in doing so, I have to ask you if you've ever had a day of fun in your life.

—*In memoriam*, Bill Ripley, 1945 – 2006

6

The Year of the Thunderbolt

Muscat called me from the operating room late Tuesday night and said that because he was on call until six a.m. and had Wednesday off, and because, since it wasn't a weekend, the nanny would be coming tomorrow to look after Rachel while his wife was at work, and because it was the best snow year since the nineteenth century, and because he was crazy, yes, he would climb and ski the Thunderbolt with me on a one-day lunatic ski excursion from New York City. As he told me this I imagined him wrestling an immense hypodermic into the jugular of yet another unconscious victim of Brooklyn gang-warfare, a procedure Muscat has told me is one of the most interesting in anesthesiology. So what if it was 175 miles each way, Paul continued, or that we had to be back by dinnertime or risk being terminated with extreme prejudice by our wives and psychologically scarring his two-year-old daughter, who would grow up thinking daddy loved Mr. Raimer more than her? So what if the weathermen were predicting an arctic February cold front to sweep through the region tomorrow? So what if we didn't know where the trailhead was? We knew which mountain it was on. I packed my bags and hit the sack.

Mt. Greylock, the highest peak in Massachusetts, sits just south of Williamstown, near where the Massachusetts, New York, and Vermont borders come together. At 3,491 feet, it doesn't exactly scrape the sky, but after Mt. Washington, Katahdin, Mt. Mansfield and Camel's Hump, Greylock offers some of the best backcountry skiing in New England, on trails cut specifically for the sport many decades ago. As all those other mountains are many hours further north, Greylock stands as the best and biggest backcountry prize in the region.

The king of Greylock ski trails is the Thunderbolt, a steep, twisting trail that drops down the eastern slope from summit to valley, a sustained pitch of 2,300 feet. Like many early ski trails, it was cut by the Civilian Conservation Corps (CCC) in the 1930s, and became the site of major competitions in the years before lifts. When that innovation came in, most of the original "A" racing trails cut in the east by the CCC, such as Mt. Mansfield's Perry Merrill and Nose Dive, and New Hampshire's Wildcat Trail and Cannon's Taft Trail, were incorporated into lift-served ski areas. This didn't happen to the Thunderbolt, which never saw anything other than a small, long-dismantled lift near the bottom, and a ski area off to its south side that went belly up years ago. Although it is starting to grow in, the trail remains a backcountry classic.

Greylock is small but looms large in America's early consciousness of the mountains. Emerson counseled Thoreau when Thoreau revealed he was planning to climb it that it was a "serious mountain." When Thoreau did go, in 1844, he wrote about sleeping at the summit under a door he'd found off its hinges in an abandoned shack, and the beauty of the view across the tops of the valley fog at dawn. Although we don't know if he ever climbed it,

Melville dedicated *Pierre* to the largest mountain he could see from his house just north of Pittsfield, comparing it to a king in purple robes. There's even an eccentric theory that the mountain's outline, clad in the clouds that give it its name, resembles . . . a great, white whale.

Although I grew up in the Massachusetts Berkshires and skied almost every lift in the range as a boy in the 1960s and 1970s, in those days very few people went into the backcountry to ski. I had heard of the Thunderbolt, but never skied it. For one thing, in many of those years the snow that had once been so reliable developed the annoying habit of turning into rain before it reached the earth. So that February, when blizzard after blizzard buried southern New England and I found myself the proud possessor of a strong tele-mark turn cultivated in the Wasatch, I vowed it would be the Year of the Thunderbolt. All I needed to do was convince some other fool to make the trek with me. Enter Muscat.

Bleary-eyed from another desperate night of sewing people back together, Paul picked me up at seven on Monday, and, dressed almost as strangely as the hookers on 10th Avenue (albeit more warmly), we sped north on the Taconic Parkway. About three hours later, we were nosing around on unmarked roads at the base of the mountain, searching for the trailhead. After parking and then thrashing around in the woods, we finally found it, tucked into an unmarked drainage at the corner of a field that was once the finish area for races.

The snow was copious. There were no tracks, and we took turns breaking trail, sinking in a foot on each step. It was deep, it was dry, it had no raincrust or wind damage, and it was one hell of a workout with only two people. As we wound our way up through the forest we began to realize that the weatherman had, for once, been right. Clouds were rippling the summit like prayer flags and when we stopped for lunch at a shelter about halfway up, we were cold in minutes. The fettuccine alfredo I had cooked for dinner the night before had congealed into frozen ganglia. It was disgusting to watch Paul eat his portion. Perhaps living so close to death on a daily basis has ruined his table manners. I have no such excuse.

Climbing New England trails is different from climbing above treeline, east or west, or even in the pine and aspen forests of the lower slopes of the Rockies. Again excepting Mt. Washington, Katahdin, and a few other isolated slide paths on the highest peaks, avalanche is never a problem, but views are rare and the terrain tends to buck and roll. Trails twist in every direction as they cross the folds of hollows and drainages. Successful touring in the east is less a question of picking a safe line to a ridge or summit, than of reading the maps carefully enough to make sure you're on the right trail, as many of the best trails for skiing (or gaining access to the ski trails) are poorly marked, and rarely have lead tracks. Seclusion has its advantages. At one point we flushed a wild turkey from the brush. It lumbered off through the bare branches like a laden B-52.

We decided not to skin the upper half of the trail, to save the snow and to avoid the steep grade, but ascended another ski trail with more switchbacks, the Bellows Pipe Trail. After seven switchbacks through deepening snow, we joined the Appalachian Trail, which runs across the top of both the Thunderbolt and Bellows Pipe as it descends northwards from the summit. Unsure of how far a walk it would be if we stayed on the deep snow of the AT, we decided to cross over the ridge a few hundred feet, then walk up the unplowed auto road. Big mistake. Although the snow had been compacted by snowmobilers, the road climbs very, very gradually, circling the summit cone almost twice before arriving. The light was beginning to fade, and the snowy hills below us and out to the Taconic Range to the west, the Berkshires to the south and east, and the Green Mountains to the north, began to dapple in the blues and oranges that come with sub-zero temperatures.

The summit is bald, and once there, we confronted serious

weather, single-digit cold and high winds combining to drop the
chill factor into the forty- to fifty-below range. Bascom Lodge, the
old Appalachian Mountain Club shelter, was boarded up tight, so
there was no escape from gusts strong enough to send unattended
ski poles skittering across the ice. As Paul came onto the summit I
could see from fifty feet that his nose was white, a problem we fixed
with a warm hand, but we had taken much longer than expected
on the climb, we were tired, and it was time to get down.

When the weather is that harsh, there has to be an implicit understanding of what needs to be done at every moment. Doctors are
good at that. Hunkered down in the wind-shadow of the lodge, with
hardly a word, we strapped on knee pads, adjusted laces and buck-
les, and coaxed frozen zippers. After scrabbling across the summit,
we descended the Appalachian Trail to the north, and as soon as we
dropped into the woods, the snow improved and the wind calmed.
By the time we'd descended the four hundred feet to the hard right-
turn onto the Thunderbolt, we were gliding through squeaky cold
snow over a foot deep, light and dry on a cushion thick enough to
cover the chest-high brambles and saplings of summer. We made
the turn onto the first steep pitch of the Thunderbolt proper, and
the trail rolled away to the valley, a secret, unbroken stash of white
in the late afternoon shadow, two thousand verts without a track
in sight. The wind swirled in the treetops.

The first two pitches after the turn are the steepest, somewhere
in the 35-degree range. After several hundred vertical feet it backs
off, but still falls away nicely, a classic New England ski run. The
designers knew their game and built in switchbacks, fall-away turns,
open slopes with sudden views across the valley and multiple tran-
sitions in fall-line. To race it packed out and rutted must have been
a long, fast, technical ride.

Accompanied by the ghosts of racers, we made hundreds of
turns, the longest powder run I've ever had in New England. We

forgot how cold we were and that the light was failing as we played through pitch after pitch of winter forest. When we approached the bottom, we traversed out to the abandoned ski area. Stumbling through the woods for a few minutes brought us out onto the gentle, open fields of the lower slopes. We coasted down to the car as darkness fell.

Now all we had to do was thaw out, find some food, and get home. As we drove through downtown Adams, the thermometer on the bank read twelve degrees. When we stopped in a diner to eat, we looked the way we felt, but they fed us anyway. Paul came up with the inspired idea of calling each other's wives to say we would be several hours late, the theory being that when each woman first heard her husband's friend's voice, she would immediately worry that her own man had broken some vital part, and, on learning that he hadn't, would be so relieved that she would forgive all minor transgressions. It didn't work.

About halfway through dinner, Paul looked up and said, "Davecantalkneemoh," and began to slide down the orange vinyl like a junkie going into a nod. Starting to fade myself, I poured him into the car, which looked like we had recently robbed both a ski store and a fast food concession. Paul revived briefly around Poughkeepsie, insisting that when we stop for gas we buy gummy bears and apple juice in a convenience store whose fluorescent lights bit at our eyes. He still wore knee pads. Soon after that, we traversed the dark, snowless suburbs, then shot across the Harlem River onto the island of granite platforms, feeling as if we had left the natural world behind.

We've all felt it, the warp of reentering the hive after even a single day on some testing peak. And alpinists have been writing about the tension between going away and coming back for centuries. It's been there from the beginning, maybe April 26, 1336, when the Italian humanist Petrarch ascended Mt. Ventoux, in southern

France. That may be the first record we have of climbing a mountain when the only motive was the climb itself. That's the motive Petrarch claims in a famous letter he composed on the evening of the same day to his former confessor, Father Dionigi da Borgo San Sepolcro, an Augustinian monk. Petrarch's letter makes it clear, however, that he wrote to Dionigi not only to describe the joy of the excursion, but also because he was feeling guilty about the "earthly enjoyment" that the view from the summit had given him. In retrospect he decides that, like St. Augustine (whose *Confessions* he carried with him to the summit), he should have had his mind on more spiritual questions than his own selfish experience, berating himself for this lapse: "How earnestly we should strive, not to stand on mountain-tops, but to trample beneath us those appetites which spring from earthly impulses." Petrarch seems to be torn between a Renaissance desire to explore and know the world, and a medieval view that such knowledge is irrelevant, that what he should have understood from the start is that

> nothing is wonderful but the soul, which, when great itself, finds nothing great outside itself. Then, in truth, I was satisfied that I had seen enough of the mountain; I turned my inward eye upon myself, and from that time not a syllable fell from my lips until we reached the bottom again.

Well—maybe he was just tired, hungry and cold. But Petrarch's encounter with the mountain convinced him that what is most worth contemplating was not what he had seen from the summit, but rather what lay within his own soul.

Before you decide that Petrarch's reaction against enjoying the beauty of the natural world has nothing to do with the way we live now, consider how earnestly and anxiously we still defend our recreation against arguments that it is only a frivolous and selfish entertainment. But no, we say, perhaps a bit testily, wait a minute, to love the world's wild garden, especially its ragged, magnificent edges, its roaring green waves, its craggy peaks, is a good in itself. Here in the modern world, perhaps especially in America, we have an outdoors made available to us in philosophy and in reality as a transcendent vision. Our encounters with it can be a communion with the sources of creation, part of life rather than an escape from it.

But perhaps we protest too much. Maybe the anxiety we feel between wildness and polis is productive, even useful, an achievement, not a problem. Petrarch might not have had his vision of God that day unless he had climbed Ventoux. The complexity of drawing these two things together—our purposeless joy in nature on one hand, our purposeful obligations on the other—shows how much we remain Petrarch's ambivalent heirs.

Odd how the wilderness and the city, whether of man or of God, give each other meaning. And so I remember: tired humanists, friends for life, we rattled down the West Side Highway, rack after rack of glittering lights on our left, the rotting docks on our right, fragments of wilderness in our hair, smelling bad, contemplating sleep and tomorrow's work, touched by delight and the frigid wind and swirling snow of the Thunderbolt.

7

Sixteen Turns

Life, friends, is meaningless. As mammals with overdeveloped brains, we have devised all sorts of ways to help us avoid noticing this fact, and unfortunately, many of these supreme fictions, these obsessions—money, power, religion, science, philosophy, vodka, sex—can become destructive. I have my own little tricks that I hope are more gentle and life-affirming. One of them is to go skiing at least one day every month. Not every month of the ski season—every month of the year. Every year. I have a little book where I record such adventures. As I said, it's an obsession.

Any sissy can ski from November to April. And if you're an even moderately committed backcountry skier, May and June are easy, even in New England. July and October are easy in the Rockies and other big ranges of the west. The real test in this part of the hemisphere comes from August and September. Oh, you could fly to Argentina or New Zealand, or go ride the lifts at Mt. Hood, and in my strict accounting I would allow that, but in your heart you'd know it verges on cheating. And pouring a cooler of melting beer ice out on the driveway and then jumping up and down on it doesn't count. Same for sand skiing or those Nordic jump ramps made out of recycled toothbrushes, or tilted carpets, roller blades, water skis and other ersatz technologies. No, it has to be real snow, snow that fell from the sky. And sliding on sneakers is not enough. You must go to the mountains and hump real gear for miles to find some lonely, dirt-smeared patch of avalanche debris tucked into a north-facing scree field at twelve thousand feet. Like the best art, your effort must be an extravagant and superfluous act of beauty, a way of writing your name in water for its own sake. Your own little rebellion against the darkness that surrounds us.

As a result of this kind of thinking there we were, Lance and I, on September 9th, far above Telluride, above even the Tomboy mine, just below Imogene Pass in Savage Basin, climbing a north-facing patch of what some people would call snow. Graupel was blowing sideways. Waldo the Golden Retriever, who, it should be pointed out, is female, was carrying a rock in her teeth and padding up the track behind us. I would say Waldo is a goofy dog, but after all, we had taken her skiing with us in what she no doubt thought of as summer, so I guess we have little on Waldo. She was probably thinking similarly critical things about us, such as, "Why won't these guys just cut the crap and throw my rock already?" The annual Imogene Pass race had been canceled because of snow for the first time in its thirty-one years, and I had somehow convinced Lance that this would be fun. He dug out some old telemark rock skis that will someday soon be candidates for fence posts and off we went.

One of the things that intrigues me about the San Juans is the roads. In Crested Butte, we have high, skinny, steep boulder-strewn roads, but they're not like San Juan roads. Engineer Pass, Imogene Pass—these places are like trying to drive up the side of the Death Star. At a certain point whenever I drive them—especially if the weather turns—I have visions of my little green Toyota truck tumbling and bouncing into the valley while the mountain gods laugh like Noah, my four-year-old, when he's throwing his toys down the stairs.

Maybe San Juan miners were greedier than Ruby Range miners, and therefore more willing to risk death. We had mostly anthracite coal. The San Juans were different, sporting heavier metals. As we bounce along I imagine some demented, toothless drunk smiling at his pals in the bar of the Sheridan Hotel, saying, "We're gonna be rich! It's gold, I tell ya, gold!" The next day there he is, lighting dynamite fuses with a cigar, drooling tobacco juice into his beard as he and his pals blast a road out of a cliff. And not a wide road, either. Have to conserve dynamite.

So at one point in the drive up, where the road narrowed to about seventy-six inches and I couldn't see over the hood and water was spattering us from some high waterfall and another car was bearing down on us and there didn't seem to be room to pull over without falling to our death, I admit I froze like a deer in the lights of an oncoming semi. Lance glanced over at my bloodless knuckles; in his typically gentle and calm way, he offered to drive, and I said, "Uh, sure." Actually, it was worse than that. I think what I did was squeak, "Lance! How about you drive?"

It wasn't the first time that summer I'd gone in search of snow. On July 12, Jeff Scott and I had driven up a more reasonable mining road onto the shoulder of Mt. Owen, a thirteen thousand-foot peak just west of Crested Butte. Owen is home to the Gunbarrel Couloir, a steep, straight shot that faces more or less north and fills with spindrift in the winter. In a good year it holds snow well into August, providing up to eight hundred vertical feet of steep skiing that cuts through the wildflowers like a lost soapsud.

The Rubies form the westernmost ramparts of the Rockies around Crested Butte. From their summits you can look out to Grand Mesa, the Utah Desert, and on a clear day the La Sals, which must be a hundred miles away. The sky was azure, glacier lilies were waving in the breeze, puffy white clouds were sailing by, and we were skiing right through the heart of it all, floating down a ribbon of dense névé in a dream of summer. I've forgotten the details of thousands of days on the lifts. They all blend together. I'll never forget that day with Jeff.

One of the beauties of summer skiing is the snow. In the winter, especially in the Rockies, things get tender. I generally stay off the high peaks in the colder months, when the snowpack is unstable and large quantities of it have a disturbing habit of migrating quickly to the valley. Spring skiing—late March to mid-June—is the very best part of the season in Colorado, the time when almost anything that holds snow becomes skiable. The major rule in this case is that once things have begun to warm up and stabilize, there has to be a good freeze at night and you have to be skiing before it gets too warm. Hit it right and it's like surfing the bubbles on a tilted glass of champagne for thousands and thousands of vertical feet—but you get only one run, because after the window of warming passes it all turns to slop. In the summer, the runs are shorter, but the snow has become so dense that it is safe and fun to ski at any time of day. It has a different texture than spring corn, more like crushed felt, and it holds that consistency for hours. Heaven.

I must be quite far gone, as I don't know why so many people find the idea of this kind of behavior odd. I remember skiing Blue Peak, above Independence Pass, one year in June a decade ago with Muscat. He'd come to Denver for a medical convention and I convinced him to take a break from dissecting pickled cadavers and make some turns. We met before dawn at the pass and headed up. The first run was unforgettable—thousands of feet of corn snow as smooth as a senator. We were dressed in full battle gear crossing the road for a second lap on terrain that faced North and hadn't yet warmed up. Boots, poles, packs, skis over our shoulders. The snowbanks were six feet high by the road. The sun was up and the travelers had arrived to stop and ogle. People who, in my view, were dressed for immediate hypothermia, in T-shirts and shorts, would stare at us and say things like "What y'all doing?" and "Are you guys going skiing?" How do you answer such a question without sounding like a sarcastic jerk? "Sorry, ma'am, we're on high alpine prison trash detail and we're not allowed to talk . . . "

In my humble opinion, skiing is the thing to do if you're in a place where there is snow on the ground. Just because the high school calendar indicates that it's time for baseball or they're playing golf back home is no reason to capitulate to the sports marketers. I live in Colorado and I'll go skiing whenever I damn well please.

Summer skiing does have some specific dangers. It's important to check out the gravity side of the snow/rock interface. If it's at any kind of odd or significant angle, and it often is, you need to be confident of that final turn. Once when I was young and even more foolish, I was skiing with my wife Emily and our friend Bruce at St. Mary's Glacier (a permanent snowfield—there are no glaciers in Colorado, just as there's no such thing as a "crested butte." It's a pointed laccolith, but that's what you get when you let drunk miners name stuff, although I have to admit that Pointed Laccolith probably wouldn't make a good name for a town). St. Mary's is a popular summer spot to the north of Idaho Springs, not far from I-70. Near the bottom I was making turns back and forth across a rounded slope transition. The feeling of weightlessness between turns was delicious, the flatter pitch on my left, the steep one falling away to the rocks on my . . . oops. Bruce said he watched me accelerate head first, sans helmet, into the boulders and started wondering about EMS response times. Apparently people have died doing this at St. Mary's. I came up laughing and merely scratched, but when he skied over, he was a distinctly whiter shade of pale.

There are local summer ski spots like this all over Colorado. Aspen has Independence Pass for the early summer, then Snowmass

Bowl and Montezuma, on the side of Castle Peak, for the later months. Telluride has Savage Basin. Crested Butte has the Gunbarrel, Yule Pass, and the north side of Mt. Justice. Breckenridge has the 4th of July Bowl on Peak 10. Vail has . . . well, I don't know, parking structures and golf courses.

That day in the graupel with Lance and Waldo we got to the snowpatch and looked at it and Lance said, "It was a lot bigger a few months ago" and we both laughed and started walking. The weather closed in again. We were at the top in just a few minutes, put on our skis and got sixteen turns in about four inches of wet new snow on top of the old snowfield. I loved it. Waldo was happy to see some action, even if we didn't throw her rock. Lance was laughing. I have to believe we were some of the only people in America skiing that day. The few, the proud, the obsessed. The alive.

Two weeks later we had one of the biggest early-season storms I've ever seen in Colorado. The high peaks were buried, so on September 23 I drove as high as I could up Washington Gulch, parked, and climbed up above the abandoned mining town of Elkton to about 11,800' on the shoulder of Mt. Baldy. At treeline there was 18" of heavy snow, with even more up high, but I opted for the gentle meadows below treeline rather than the femur-busting rocks above. I skied more than fifteen hundred feet of gentle hillsides back down to the car, scores of good turns, bouncing through the grass tips. I gently bottomed out four times while spiraling down through aspen meadows filled with swirling gold and green leaves.

When I got back to town and told a few friends who'd spent the day doing exciting things like cleaning the garage or complaining about how they couldn't go biking, or working out on a Stairmaster at the gym, they looked at me oddly and said things like, "I'm not ready to think about that yet," or, more to the point, "You're nuts."

I just smiled. There are none so blind as those who will not see. October is going to be great.

Interlude

God's Lost Tomatoes

—Composed *in situ extemporare en pleine aire mit*
Lance Waring, *il miglior montagnardo*

Forced outside one night in Telluride
With our cigars, bad jokes, poignant mustard,
Lawn chairs and whisky
In the pouring rain,
We lounged under the roof near the Freebox,
Smoking and eating sliced tomatoes.

The tomatoes
Were not from Telluride,
Were not from the Freebox,
Nor was the hot mustard,
That made our tears run like rain
Until we drank more whisky.

The cigars mixed with the whisky,
The spice with our tomatoes,
The snow with the rain
That night in Telluride,
When Mr. Mustard
Met us at the Freebox.

That stupid Freebox
Made us guzzle all the whisky!
Then the wild mustard
Spanked all the tomatoes
Into the smoky sinuses of Telluride
As we tramped home with our lawn chairs in the rain.

And despite the rain,
Despite the poor pickings in the Freebox,
We remained in Telluride
Nursing our wet cigars and whisky,
Imagining other, distant tomatoes
With which to swill mustard.

O fragrant mustard!
O lovely rain!
O willing cigars, tomatoes!
We were the Freebox!
We understood the perfect whisky!
We were happy in Telluride!

That night in Telluride, we welcomed every mustard.
Jah shared our cigars and whisky, we traded hats in the rain.
And now we will always inhabit the Freebox, like God's lost
    tomatoes.

8

The Lots

In those days little did I think, and little did I think that one day I would back a rented Ford Escort up to the door of that beat-up Smith College office building still standing at the base of the long loading ramp that leads to some old dorm at Clarke School for the Deaf, and remember this: this place, this ramp and hill-tilted interconnected web of parking lots that pass hard by the final home of his projects was where, so long ago, one lazy afternoon after another, waves of dog-day heat rising from the angled tar, I would hike to the top with my simple board, so much less than the big fat rides now sported by my students as they commute across the Boulder campus like the fabulous and beautiful punks they are, to class.

Back then, utterly alone under my own lonely heat wave, I would push off and start to arc tight GS turns because I knew what was coming, dropping down the ramp of Round Hill, facing almost due south toward Elm Street, West Street, South Street, and then beyond the edge of town the Ox Bow, Chicopee, Hartford, Long Island and ultimately Venezuela, though what did I know or care of that, launching sans helmet down that dock ramp on my small orange skateboard into the three weekend-empty lots resplendent with potential energy of seventy-five-vertical-foot serendipitous blacktop sporting do-or-die corners. Right there I learned I was on my own, a lover healthy as a happy swallow in my desires and not fastened to squat, but in fact and deed a mortal animal utterly alive. The polyurethane wheels began to sing with a poise, with a balance and a commitment to gravity that is definitely no place for parents, let alone old philosophers, although they might stand as I did in that recollection, holding a box of books, recalling how back then, just as I passed the last office my father ever occupied, I had to make that first heel-side left-handed right-angle corner to the east into the first lot which, if a single car had ever appeared would have rewarded me with bone crunching geometry but, because this was Saturday, lay empty as a windsock. I tightened the line, leaned back, rocked and rocketed over the parking space lines passing under my ten hung toes like picket fenceposts, and where it angled for the blind lip into parking lot number two, I absorbed it and dropped, pressing down to maintain contact with the earth like Antaeus over that dark roller, cranking another hard heelside ninety-degrees into true north at hyper-wobble. The hot air parted around me and my sliver of frantic plastic passed through it so perfectly that I thought I might leave the planet and soar away on the principle that total pressure is constant everywhere in a fluid flow.

Yet in those days, I remained terrestrial and pulled a full heelside loop to bleed speed in the northern end of the lot, a shallow bowl around a drain, for if I had shot straight to the final lip into the coda of parking lot three with that much momentum, I'd have launched like a tomato from a catapult into Henshaw Avenue, but after that heelside drain loop I could then drop the final roller and arc into a final toe-side curl, heading south once more in lot number three, slowly rolling back around north while dismounting to a jog, blissful as some artist who has just hucked himself into the void, only to grab the board, still rolling, and head back for the top.

And you can bet about six inches of obliterated forearm skin (three, doubled) I still remember the hot afternoon when I misjudged the drain loop vector in lot two, couldn't calm the harmonic wiggle of my wicked, spastic plank and planted my front wheels in the square holes of the drain at velocity, which made the world go very, very quiet as I continued but the board did not, airborne, like an angel of summer floating briefly free above the frozen tar, almost unsurprised until perhaps a dozen or so feet and what seemed like a month later I landed as luckily as anyone could, head up, arms out, and ground to a raw halt on that asphalt. I wore the awesome scabs for weeks.

Now decades later at the base of the ramp, where it turns down east into lot one, there I stood, my father gone, carrying his books out of that office, the dusty office where he went to document the unheralded alienation of the elites, and where he went less and less as Parkinson's slowed him to a crawl, still never knowing—because indifferent to—the joy I once lay down outside it long ago.

In retrospect, it resembled the pointless, beautiful search for an odd, perfect number, the way I roared alone past what would one day be his final office to prove the glory of gravity, summer afternoons in those desolate lots. I wonder where the light that time reflected and the light that shone from it is now, as it travels and disperses towards the Pleiades.

9

Tonic of Taconic

This story begins with yet another phone call, in the darkest hours of a Tuesday night, from the backcountry-obsessed anesthesiologist Dr. Paul Muscat. He was speaking to me in a hushed voice somewhere near the operating room: "I have a very sick patient, there's blood everywhere, it's disgusting, I can only talk for a minute, are we skiing tomorrow or what?" I told him that he was the sick one, but that, since he asked, I knew for a fact that there had been so much snow that we could go for the abandoned Taconic Trails Ski Area and the Williams College Ski Trail, even though it was already early April. "Excellent," he said. *Click.* The following morning I picked him up a bit after seven and we headed north. Literally sticking to our principle that you can only ski well if you eat grease, we choked down some Egg McMuffins and hash browns as we wove our way onto the Taconic.

The last time I skied the Williams College Ski Trail—maybe one of the last times it was skiable, for there was never any snowmaking on it—had been as a college sophomore in February of . . . well, a long time ago. It was one of the most exciting courses I ever saw in over a decade of racing, almost 1,400' of drop, which began as a very narrow but gentle, twisting trail, then grew steeper and steeper, throwing blind and fallaway turns at the accelerating racer, until the trail took a sharp left turn and dumped out onto a wide, straight shot (the slalom hill) that dropped several hundred feet at more than 35°. Fast. The trail never saw a lift to the top, although there was at that time a pony lift, now long gone, that carried skiers up the lower, steepest third. From there, just as in the old days, you had to hoof it to the summit. After the Thunderbolt, it is the longest serious trail in Massachussetts, with several hundred more feet of drop than anything off the lifts at any area.

The trail lies in a steep valley around which cluster the highest peaks of the Taconics, a small, steep range that runs down the border between New York and Massachusetts. Although it is across a valley to the east, Greylock is technically part of this range, not the Berkshires, and the bald summit of Berlin Mt., where the Williams trail begins, offers a big view of Greylock's summit and western aspect, a rippling bear shoulder of forest.

As luck would have it, the nearby abandoned Taconic Trails ski area is connected to the top of Berlin Mt. by a poorly maintained trail called the Taconic Crest Trail. The ski area, which went out of business long ago, had one of the highest base elevations in New England—two thousand feet—nothing to sneer at when every inch can make a difference in the local quest for snow. While many of the trails are growing in, there is still plenty of room to ski, and a good day will find the old parking lot filled with cars as local backcountry skiers and riders climb for their turns. Few of these people know about the Williams trail and how to get to it, and that trail, while accessible from its base, would be a rough climb on skins because of the grade. Besides, the Taconic Crest trail is beautiful, and skiing it turns the excursion into a circuit instead of a simple up and down affair.

A mere 175 miles from home, we started up the New York side of Route 2, which crosses into Massachusetts right at the base of the ski area, at Petersburg Pass. The storm that had dumped an inch of cold rain in New York City and southern New England had turned to snow just below this pass, and in the parking lot we found several inches of fluff on top of a glacier-like bed of utterly consolidated snow several feet deep. Just fifteen hundred feet below us, the valleys were brown with maple bark and dead, sodden grass, but here the progress of the storm, changing from snow to ice to rain and then back to snow, had not only saved the snowpack, but grown two-inch rime on every exposed branch, making the forest a labyrinth of delicate white thorns.

The base was so firm and grippy underneath the new snow that we could walk on it. Near the top of the area, where the Taconic Crest trail cuts away to the south, we couldn't resist dumping our packs and taking a quick run before heading on. The turning was so easy that it seemed like cheating. The snow underneath was smooth and consistent, the upper few inches a bed of pliant feathers.

As the sun tried to cut through the breaking remnants of the storm, we headed down to Berlin Pass, a challenge, as the trail is so narrow, then up the long, gentle ridge to the summit of Berlin Peak several miles away. The walking on this part of the trail is usually easy, as snowmobilers come up from the New York side to ride the trail. It's a quiet stroll through the woods up a steady but easy grade that climbs the narrow crest of the range, and the reward, after about forty-five minutes, is the bald, 2,700-foot summit, which can offer hundred-mile views of the Berkshires, Taconics, Catskills, Greens, and even the distant outline of the Adirondack high peaks region. The day we were there, Greylock was fading in and out of the clouds that swirled in the wake of the storm, and a few snow-flakes sparkled in the April light.

As on the Thunderbolt and so many other New England tours,

you need to have a good map to figure out exactly where to go on this expedition, as some sections are poorly marked, if at all. Without cartographic help, unwary skiers might wind up thrashing about in the woods until, overcome by confusion, they would sink down upon a broken log, weeping, never more to rise. With a bit of planning and cunning, however, you can coax the trails from the forest. The head of the Williams trail is only a pole's throw from the summit of Berlin Mt., and coming upon that abandoned trail to find all the brush buried under an utterly untracked, smooth blanket made us feel like we'd hit the lottery. Backcountry skiers know this feeling well. We should coin a word for it, a variation of serendipity. This word would define the sensation of having worked and traveled hard, praying for good snow and fresh tracks, and then finding that weather, snow, timing, and camaraderie can come together into a single element. We knew that every turn was going to be as sweet as an unexpected tax refund.

And it was. I'd skied the trail in December, in deep, unconsolidated snow tracked up by snowboarders, and that had been a wrestling match. This time it was like flying home. The saplings and brush were shut down under as much as four feet of ice with a smooth, creamy surface. Turn after turn, as the trail churned and steepened, was effortlessly silky. Paul and I hooted and hollered our way down into the small, empty valley.

Paul is an accomplished alpinist with a number of first ascents in North America, but this had been his first year of serious skiing, and at one point I turned around and saw his skis behaving differently than they ever had, beginning to arc like bows under his feet as he found the sweet spot and jumped on it every time, his hands forward, pole plants connecting like clockwork. What a pleasure to see a friend figuring it out. I could sense his intent, practically feel him locking in on the concept. Maybe someday he'll teach me how not to puke my guts out as we approach the summit of some unclimbed peak in the Yukon.

As for me—as we descended, I remembered the intensity and crowds of the races I'd run there, the intensity of the fall-away turns on hardpack at forty miles per hour. With the trail starting to grow in, the buildings vanished, and all those boys and girls scattered into their adult lives, it seemed like a long time ago. Still, in the intervening years, I had changed more than the hill. My knees had changed a lot more.

At the bottom, where the snow had softened in the old finish area, we met some local skiers trying to post hole their way up. I couldn't imagine they'd make it, and they didn't, turning around about halfway up the lowest pitch. Meanwhile, Paul and I went over to the old seventy-meter jump to see if the outrun was still skiable. It had grown in, and the narrow path we could have skied was too steep to climb straight up in the soft snow, so we let it go. We hiked out on the old Boston Post Road, which crosses Berlin Pass, reversing the progress of our descent as we passed through spring snow to firm snowpack and finally back up into the ethereal region of rime. At the pass we met the Taconic Crest Trail, closing the circle of our own tracks.

We nabbed another five hundred-foot drop run from the top of the old ski area to the parking lot. There are still several routes that haven't grown in at the ski area, and while most are gentle, several have a sustained pitch. We hollered and hooted again, back to the old, virtually empty parking lot.

We arrived at the car about six hours after we had left. Our gear jumped into the back like a dirty dog, and we headed home to the metropolis. A few days later the spring monsoon set in and washed everything left in southern New England away in the biggest runoff in years. Our names writ in water. Yet that's the way backcountry skiing is: you never know when all the necessary parts will combine to smile on your aspirations. The only way to find out is to go, to damn the torpedoes of work or lassitude, and trundle the necessary distance to the hill, squint into the light, and then begin to climb. Sometimes you find yourself eating broken glass, but sometimes angels sing the shape of serendipity from gravity, friendship, and mountain snow.

10

A Week in a Hut

You look at pictures, you read, and you watch movies about turns and avalanches and snow and mountains and climbing and gear and clothing. Sometimes this makes you forget what it's all really about. Unless you're Jimmy Faust or Greg Hill, who do occasionally climb for twenty-four hours straight, you are unlikely to spend more than eight hours a day skiing, and rarely that long. Most of the rest of the time you are doing something else. People think that you go to a backcountry hut to climb and ski, but even then, most of the time, you're doing something else: living very closely with other people and learning about them and maybe about yourself. The things you learn in such an unusual place can change you for the rest of your life.

Some of my deepest friendships were either inaugurated or greatly deepened by time in an isolated hut, in summer or winter, in the Berkshire Hills, in the White Mountains of New Hampshire, in Colorado, in British Columbia and elsewhere. Some of that mysterious change happened on the snow—all right, a lot of it happened on the snow—but even what happened there occurred in the context of so much more: traveling together; flying or hiking in; making meals, dining together, cleaning up; games of Scrabble; conversations about everything imaginable; stoking the sauna and then baking in it; carrying water and wood; telling jokes; playing music; figuring out what to do when your roommate snores (bring earplugs); sharing the outhouse; drinking; shoveling; repairing gear; and so much laughter. I've even been on hut trips where couples got engaged.

And yes, there's the climbing and the skiing. But at a certain point, what is there to say about it? It was great; it rained; it snowed every day; the trees below the hut are incredible; the trees below the hut suck; the Adamants look like shark's teeth; the snow bridges were good this year on the glacier. Of course, we go for the skiing.

Or do we? Couldn't we ski the same terrain, and a heck of a lot more of it—even terrain that is otherwise inaccessible—if we saved our pennies and flew in a bird? I remember one day at Golden Alpine Holidays. We had hiked up from the Vista Hut, over the ridge, skied a long line down into the next valley, and then we were climbing up onto Little Bear—a good walk. Perfect snow. We could hear a chopper off in the distance and our guide, Keith Webb, said that the terrain was shared with one of the local heli operations. Sure enough, there were the landing stakes on the summit; we ate lunch in their LZ. The weather was breaking down and Keith said he wouldn't be surprised if the heliskiers landed here for a run on their way back to the lodge near Rogers Pass. If we wanted the goods first, we had to go.

When we were about halfway down (it was blower/killer/sweet/phat/huge/copacetic—take your pick), the chopper came in and then, just a few minutes later, down they came. We were skiing long lines, but savoring things. After all, we'd spent the entire day earning it. The folks who came down must have pitied us. There we were, sweaty, skiing with packs, looking and smelling a bit like the Yeti; they were in full alpine regalia, one-piece suits, unburdened backs. No sign of sweat. We chatted. Nice folks. Excellent skiers. The guides knew each other. Then they were all gone, down into the valley, back into their bird and up over the horizon in thirty seconds.

I love heli skiing. I've done some. I plan to do more. But it's a different experience. We knew what mountain we were on, and what aspect. We'd spent most of the day on it. And we had all climbed it together. We helped each other out, we shared food, we savored that time. We got to know each other better than we would have if each ascent took place in a loud machine, however magnificent and powerful.

That was the Want Some, Git Some trip. "Want some? Git some," was what L. kept saying. We had all tried to get along with L. He had some endearing qualities. He was an outstanding athlete. He liked to call everyone "Boss." I'm not sure why that was endearing, but it was. The problem was that he kept doing things like challenging the guides, complaining loudly and at length about the lines we were skiing and making fun of the weaker skiers in the group. One evening somebody saw him pour a bottle full of his urine out the window of his room on the second floor. The next day he claimed he was too ill to ski; and then, while we were skiing Heartbeat, a two thousand foot vertical tube stuffed with snow on a flank a mile away from the lodge, we looked up and saw him cutting a solo track up the opposite side of the drainage.

To say our guide was speechless would not be exactly accurate. I don't think I should print the speech he did use on a page that might fall into the hands of minors.

The next day L. flew out, at the owners' expense, and everyone relaxed a bit. Many of us who met on that trip still get together, and we even have T-shirts from a trip to Selkirk Lodge that say, "Want some? Git some." The Legend of L-man lives on.

Many of the others on that trip with L. became life-long friends.

Last January, after missing a couple of years of hut-skiing with them because my back was such a mess, and after diligently going to yoga class, I packed my bags and my Naproxen and headed for BC yet again, with many of them, though now with a lot of their friends too. Twenty of us flew into Ruedi Beglinger's amazing home with the usual awe. Ho hum, just another splendid view. It snowed a foot a day for a week. The high alpine was like the inside of a ping-pong ball, but we had runs in the trees, such as Excalibur, that might as well be tattooed onto my brain.

But enough of that. The situation was complicated. Ruedi had a private client that week—a great guy named Dave who owns cherry orchards in the Okanagan and knows a lot of jokes that cannot be retold here. I'd spend a week skiing with him any time. At any rate, as a result of this arrangement, Ruedi agreed to let Jim, our guide, subcontract the hut. Many of us knew each other, but others hadn't met. There was a contingent from Crested Butte, where I lived then; and one from Boulder; and a group from New Zealand, some of whom we knew from other trips; and friends from Massachusetts and the D.C. area. The group ranged from their mid-thirties to almost sixty-years-old; men and women; doctors, lawyers, judges, builders, scientists, computer programmers, businesspeople; people who had placed in the Grand Traverse and others who'd never put a skin on a ski; brothers, lovers, spouses, friends, strangers.

Justice Wild enlightened me about the New Zealand legal system. The Americans decided it was inferior to ours and declared we were going to invade. I saw a drunken Haka delivered by howling Kiwis in briefs. Bruce P., Steve and I played the Beglingers' electronic piano and we all sang songs for hours. Norman brought his banjo. Peter got so excited he started banging the silverware. I gave Ruedi's girls a piano lesson, after which I think he decided I was ok. Nank recited Keats' "On First Looking into Chapman's Homer" while skiing the Tumbledown Glacier in a whiteout. I responded with obscene limericks. I learned of all the trouble and heartache an old friend has faced in the last few years. Which didn't keep us from having a heated argument about education in the sauna. Nicoline, Ruedi's wife, ran the tightest hut kitchen I've ever seen in my life. Susan, reduced to tears by a sore knee and the tough conditions a few times, was nailing it by the end of the week. Ruedi showed us the impressive engineering on his hydropower system. Roger had a cold and could still kick my ass on every climb, which was annoying. I made a dozen new friends. And it snowed and snowed and snowed and we climbed and skied it together every day, all day. Except for the times some of us took a day off, read books, led unhurried, unencumbered conversations: no phone, no fax, no computer, no email, no video, no web, no car, no work. Pure re-creation in the deepest sense, all of it growing out of simply being there, in an alpine hut with other people who love the mountains.

I headed for home rejuvenated, grateful that my back had healed up enough to let me do this kind of thing. And how close do we all remain? A few months later Dave called from Boulder to say he and Kim would be up to Crested Butte this week and they wanted to get together. Norman, Susan, Roger, and Bruce L. were then all still living there full-time and we saw each other all the time. Roger was my family's doctor for many years; Norman contracted all the work on my home for years (a money pit—that's what I get for living in a renovated barn . . .). Susan, his wife, is a skilled and disturbingly beautiful nurse. Now that I live on the Front Range I see and ski with Bruce P. and Steve and see their families as often as I can. For a while I sat with Steve on the board of a non-profit jazz education program. And at one point a few years ago Nank and Wild and the other Kiwis somehow convinced me to blow the bank, jump on a plane, and fly to New Zealand, where they were having the best snow season in twenty-five years, to celebrate Nank's sixtieth birthday at some lodge on a mountainside God knows where. Is this just about skiing? I don't think so. Skiing—specifically backcountry climbing and riding—is the catalyst, but it is about something that goes beyond that. As much as anything I know, this activity, especially in the crucible of a backcountry hut, can bring out the best in people. On good trips, you come to form a small, temporary community that includes infinitely more than climbing, turns, eating, and sleep. At the very least, a week in a hut gives you, each time, the opportunity to discover and create that "more."

And there are a lot of terms for what that "more" might be. But I know what I call it. I call it living the life. Though at times, when I think I can get away with it, when I believe I'll be understood, when I know I'm among friends—I might even call it something more than that.

11

Baptism by Single Track

When I first moved to Crested Butte, I thought I was good on a mountain bike. I wouldn't have made any extravagant claims. But even though I'd never competed, I'd ridden in Moab and done a number of the big Crested Butte rides on summer trips. In those days, when I had to get off and walk up parts of the longer uphills, like the final traverse to Teocalli Ridge, I always had the convenient excuse of high altitude to soothe my ego. I was also used to long rides in the northeast, loops of twenty-five-plus miles off-road in hilly country. I thought I was a mountain biker.

Ha ha.

Not everyone in Crested Butte rides bikes like the crew of human lungs I happened to fall in with and whom I'm going to refer to in this chapter as "those maniacs." There are plenty of people in Crested Butte who like to go out, toodle around, smell the flowers, say things like "Look! a bluebird!" and maybe bring a picnic lunch tastier than sports bars and water. There are people who do not enjoy risking dismemberment and paralysis on two thousand-vertical-foot, rock-studded single-track descents.

Unfortunately, I rarely meet such gentle souls, at least not while in the saddle. No, when I moved to town, I met people with whom I could not keep up while going over a curb, people who clearly have a different body chemistry than I do, and for whom the innocent question, "Feel like going for a ride this afternoon?" is an invitation to grinning bedlam.

Most people who have ever ridden off-road know that Crested Butte is one of the places where the sport got its start. In the late 1970s, intrepid locals began playing around with creaky, balloon-tired junkers, adding gears, fiddling with handlebars and stems, gradually making everything stronger and lighter in an attempt to build a machine that would allow them to consume all the blood sugar in their bodies in a single day by doing things like riding to Aspen for lunch, then back for dinner. From the beginning it seems to have been just another way (like telemark skiing, which was also rediscovered in Crested Butte in the early 1970s) to get out and enjoy the beauty that surrounds the town. There's also the possibility, of course, that some locals couldn't resist the opportunity to give an aerobics lesson to certain Aspenites, but we'll let that speculation lie. From the beginning a mountain bike was not only a vehicle to get into the mountains, but also a way to enjoy adventure with friends.

Sounds corny, I know. Mountain biking has developed into such a high-tech, macho, competitive sport that it's easy to forget that it's something people usually do together. But that's the spirit that still fills most of the memorable rides I go on. The bikers in Crested Butte are so strong that there's certainly adrenalin in the air, but at the same time there is something that may seem strange to associate with such a punishing sport: manners. Yep, manners.

The fact is that many of the best riders in Crested Butte do not compete, although they may once have. They are in it for the pleasure of the ride, and most don't mind teaching you a thing or two, or giving directions, or just waiting for you if you are a slug. What matters most is the enjoyment, part natural beauty, part physical adventure, part camaraderie.

I remember one ride many years ago with John Distefano, Mike Moore, Mike Kang (the mandolin player for String Cheese Incident), Lance Waring, and a few others (memory dims beyond a certain threshold of pain). The ride we did was a classic that begins in Cement Creek, a few miles above Crested Butte South, called Reno/Flag/Bear/Dead Man's. I'm not sure exactly how long it is, but it includes three big climbs and a final descent that has more than twenty-five hairpin single-track switchbacks. I had been biking hard all summer, improving week to week, and began this ride once again with high hopes of being able to keep the others in sight.

I didn't have a chance. The majority of the times I saw them they were at rest, waiting for me. As far as I could tell, they had teleported from one resting point to the next, but it didn't seem to matter to them. On the initial climb up Reno Divide, Johny D. hung back and we chatted about his business until I got too short of breath to do anything but grunt. Of course, he was pulling wheelies while blood was coming out of my eyeballs, but still, it was a nice thing of him to do. Later in the ride, I was asking questions about the best way to position your body on the bike during a downhill, and we had a bit of a clinic on it.

Another time I was biking out of town on a trail that must remain secret. This ride begins with a very steep dirt road whose first section is tricky enough that it is almost impossible to get back on your bike if you come off. Bill and Sean, the guys I was riding with, had cleaned this tough little section and were sprinting to the top. The victim of inferior technique, I came off at about the same time as a beautiful young woman who looked like she weighed about 105 pounds. We both got back on at the same time too, and I, in a hilarious burst of masculine pride, decided that by God I would not be the last person up that hill that day.

I wasn't, but it wasn't pretty. My companion was no doubt out for an enjoyable jaunt. I, on the other hand, nearly lost my life. At the top, we all had a friendly chat where I learned that she was Kasha Rigby, probably still the best extreme telemark skier on the planet. After the ride, Bill and Sean laughed at me for about twenty minutes, taking endless joy in describing again and again the look on my face as I came around the final corner. "And then he comes around the corner and he's like—!" Cheeks puffed, eyes crossed. Cue howls.

I haven't yet done the lunch ride—the infamous ride to Aspen and back in a single day—but over the years, I have learned a few things. Some of them were technical, like how to use SPDs ("stupid pedal devices"), the pedals that attach directly to the shoe. It was a fun process, one in which I frequently found myself writhing on the ground under my bike after failing to release in a fall.

Maybe the most important lesson I've learned came to fruition on one of the last rides I took one year when I was teaching at Crested Butte Academy, a private school where I eventually became Headmaster in the 1990s. Math Department Chair Torrey Carroll, I, and a group of our students set out to ride Strand Hill, a twelve-mile loop from town, one afternoon that threatened heavy weather. One of the students, Brian, was in all the wrong clothes—baggy cotton pants, cotton shirt, on a borrowed bike that was the wrong size. Worse, he was equipped with a substantial whine. I was bringing up the rear, riding sweep, and as the rain started coming in and the track turned ugly, Brian again complained. I turned to him and gave him some kind of short, inspiring lecture along the lines of, "You can do this," and on we pedaled, into the gathering gloom.

A half an hour later, wet, muddy and tired, we reached the end of the final climb on Brush Creek Road as it curves around the shoulder of Mt. Crested Butte. The storm was passing over, a few final, gentle curtains of water dancing in the air. Somewhere to the west, the sun cut through the dissipating clouds and sculpted the most vibrant, promising, geometry of rainbow I've ever seen. Brian and I paused and watched as it framed the black, receding billows. He turned to me and said "Did I do alright?"

I told him he sure had. What a smile he gave me. We headed for town. And I'd say that was the day I became a Crested Butte mountain biker.

12

Telluride: The View from Elsewhere

Colorado ski towns are like cousins in a large, extended family. Aspen is the spoiled one who was sent off to a private school where kids snort coke in the dorms. Never learned how to do his own taxes. Vail is the one who grew up to become a Republican dentist. The others laugh at him behind his back, though he's nice enough. Breckenridge is the cute one who got a boob job even though she looked just fine. Silverthorne went to business school, figured out the high-volume/low-margin thing, then made a killing in fast food franchises. Crested Butte, where I lived for many years, prides itself on its independent funk, though these days it is a threatened funk. The town is in that phase where people show up and say, "This place is great! So laid back! The people are so friendly! There's so much charm! What do you mean I can't install an electrical snow-melt system beneath my driveway, you tree-hugging communist?"

Telluride, ah Telluride. Over the last fifteen years I've come down to Telluride many times to visit friends who introduced me to other people who became friends, to ski bumps until disk fluid squirted out of my spine, to yell, "Bope-bope!" at passing telly-dreds, to listen to great music, to contemplate log cabins on steroids. I know about a dozen people in town pretty well. I've skied in Ophir, attended Mountainfilm and given readings at the Ah Ha School for the Arts. There's even a beautiful local woman who has a private nickname for me: Pussy Dog. You're not going to learn why here, but I consider it a mark of honor. And it's not what you think.

Every time I make the turn at the bottom of the canyon and head up that improbable road snaking against red rock, I'm happy. Telluride faces the same kinds of pressures that all Colorado ski towns confront: housing prices that have gone through the roof (creating leaky houses) followed by predictable busts; bitter fights between environmentalists and people who want only the best for the valley by bulldozing it; an occasional shortage of sarcasm; the deepening crisis of second-homelessness (I myself was second-homeless for many years), and so on. But I love visiting Telluride, because I love the people I know there and the way they live.

I'm not sure why, and I don't have to be, but one story that sticks out in my mind that seems to exemplify the town was the time I came down to talk to some folks whose son had recently graduated from the private school where I was then Headmaster. I had dinner with them. They thought I was going to thank them for a recent gift to the school; I did that, but I also thought they might be interested in giving more. This is what is often referred to among people who study such things as "miscommunication." Later, they sent me a memorable letter describing my mistake. It was a learning experience.

After dinner, feeling dejected, I went back to Lance's, where I was staying. He had recently moved out of a little cabin that could best be described as an indoor-camping situation and into a place he had renovated, getting his toe into the local real estate market.

It was late fall, and a cold rain began to fall. In the dark we could
tell that somewhere not too far above the valley floor it was snowing. This made me feel better already.

For some reason I had brought fine cigars. Lance provided the
single malt and as a late-night snack we dug out crackers, fresh
tomatoes, and hot mustard. We couldn't smoke in the house, but
we wanted those cigars. To avoid the rain, we took some battered
lawn chairs down the street and sat under the awning near the Free
Box, smoking, drinking, and nibbling. It was only a few degrees
above freezing, so I dug a sweater out of the box and we talked
and laughed at the world's ironies. Ha.

Despite the ugly off-season weather, it was a weekend night
and folks were out. Lance has lived in Telluride for more than
twenty years and knows everyone, and everyone who wandered
by stopped to chat and marvel at our odd behavior. We had one
pleasant conversation after another as people absent-mindedly
rifled through old clothing, battered shoes, mysterious pieces of
electronic machinery, and so on. After our cigars were gone and we
grew cold, we trundled home and wrote a sestina together about
the evening that was eventually published in a literary journal in
Idaho. We made a small fortune on it, invested wisely in a hedge
fund, and have now both retired.

It's hard to say why some memories linger so powerfully and
definitively. But there was something about that evening that always
comes back to me when I think of it. It somehow seemed perfect,
utterly Telluridean. The quiet, the dark, the rain, the whiskey, the
relaxed feeling of friendship—no doubt these things can occur in
any small town. But they don't usually come together in front of
a pile of communal junk where everyone is excited about standing
around in bad weather.

The spirit of a place has little to do with glossy advertisements
for anything. It is a kind of ghost made up of uncountable moments

and events both public and private, human and non-human. It is weather, architecture, geology, history, flora and fauna, politics, a certain smell in the air, all of it flowing together like a river, unified yet always changing. No one can see it whole, but there's a certain point where it fixes itself in the mind as more than a collection of facts and becomes something that gives life sweetness and meaning.

Red rock. Depth-hoar. Dreds. Society Turn. Mountainfilm. Plunge. Gold Hill. Bear Creek. AC power. Lance, KB, Lise, Mark, Karin, Ernie, Kristen, Seth, Sick Liverman, Art, Rosemerry, Gus, Rhonda, Sean. The valley floor. Bluegrass. Creek surfing. The Drunken Frenchman.

Freebox mustard whiskey cigar rain sestina tomatoes lawn-chairs smoke laughter friendship . . .

All of which remind me of Lance, who skis like a ball of mercury gliding down hill; whom I have seen drop his pack at the top of a climb and hustle back down the trail to help others; who came skiing with me in a snow squall in early September to make sixteen turns in Savage Basin; who is a gifted teacher and writer and who walks his talk; who is the godson of my sons . . . man, am I lucky to have a friend like that.

Who lives in Telluride.

13

Carving the Big One

Lou Dawson, Zack Stenson, Paul Gallaher, and I were standing on the edge of a nameless, obsidian-smooth lake, gazing up at the shimmering wall of corn in Mt. Elbert's Box Creek Cirque. We'd all stuck the 50° crux and now was the time to tell ourselves how good we were.

While I could justifiably claim to have been the most terrified, with my ankles flapping in the thin air, Lou announced that nineteen-year old Zack may have earned bragging rights to the first-ever snowboard descent of the Cirque. And Lou Dawson, the first person ever to ski from the summits of all fifty-four Colorado peaks over fourteen thousand feet, should know, if anyone does—his 1994 book, *Dawson's Guide to Colorado Fourteeners*, is still the Bible of the high Colorado backcountry. So Zack, despite all the teasing he took for carrying an airplane wing up a mountain, had been the most original, and on his first ever descent of a Colorado fourteener.

Only calendar slaves think that the ski season ends April. It never really ends, and in the backcountry that's just when the best skiing opens up in Colorado. Afternoons return, rivers roar back to life, and sometime in May or June the high dirt roads melt out, avalanche danger diminishes, and the real ski season begins. In a big year, epic descents are possible well into July. And so it was that I found myself, at three a.m. on June 25 that spring, stumbling around the Half Moon campground just outside of Leadville, preparing to grunt my telemark skis 4,350 feet to the top of one of America's larger mountains.

Our primary goal was to have a ripping good time, but we looked like a team of multiglisse scientists about to investigate the world of gravity: my former student Zack Stenson had his board, Lou and Paul Gallaher were on alpine-touring gear, and I had brought my telemark setup. After teasing Zack for carrying four acres of p-tex, we watched in amazement as Lou downed what he called "the mountaineer's breakfast" (coffee and aspirin). Then we started up the trail, stumbling over the beams of our headlamps.

At 14,433 feet, Elbert is the highest peak in the entire Rocky Mountain chain, and the second highest in the lower forty-eight, surpassed only by California's Mt. Whitney. Yet Elbert is an oddly tame climb, if a long one. You don't have to be a great athlete, though being stubborn helps. There is a clearly marked, gentle trail all the way to the summit, with no typical Rocky Mountain scree fields, and that makes it a test of will, not skill. It's mostly a long, beautiful trudge. If you're lucky, and follow all the important rules for keeping body and soul together, the reward in late spring can be huge, exhilarating skiing.

Below treeline the trail is buffed like a toll road, and we followed it up about six hundred vertical feet before turning right and bushwhacking a more direct line up a gentle ridge laced with old snowbanks. By the time we broke free of the trees at about 11,600 feet, the sun was up and we found ourselves strolling through a meadow covered with hardy plants testing the promise of spring with delicate pink and yellow flowers. The night before had frosted hard, promising great skiing in a few hours, there was no wind, and the only sound was the internal combustion of our hearts and lungs as we vectored up.

There's nothing like emerging from the trees at dawn on a mountain as big as Elbert. This is where skis strapped to a pack stop getting caught in branches and the high alpine tundra begins. The view toward the hidden summit, still almost three thousand feet up, not only filled me with awe, but also gratitude for engineers who have worked so hard to bring us lightweight gear.

We regrouped, got back on the trail, and started up the spine of the ridge, which was clear of snow but surrounded by huge snowfields on either side. We were able to use the trail in sections and had to climb snow in others, although this was, as Lou likes to say, a *no-brainer*, as the shoulder of the mountain is never more than moderately pitched, the line is obvious, and the surface smooth. Also, the late spring was a boon to all of us, especially Zack, as frozen corn requires no skins or snowshoe slogging—everyone walks with gear on the back. At the same time, it was great fun to watch Zack become more and more hypoxic with every step. Age and experience have their prerogatives; at least I was able to get far enough ahead so that when I had to stop and whimper for breath, he couldn't see me.

Taking what was, for him, a leisurely pace, Lou summited at about 9:15. Unlike Lou, who is part gazelle, I climb like a mule, continually reminding myself that it's not real pain pounding in my temples, just aerobic distress, so I was twenty minutes behind and the others arrived soon after.

After we had gulped some calories and could see straight, what we saw was that we were on top of the neighborhood. To the east, Leadville glinted across the valley and 4,200 feet down, against the Mosquito Range; to the south, the jagged Collegiates marched toward Buena Vista; directly to the north stood Mt. Massive

(Colorado's second-highest peak) and other ranges far beyond; and to the west, across the continental divide and down toward Aspen and the Elk Mountains, was a geological jigsaw of immense mountains, among them Capitol, Snowmass, the Maroon Bells, Pyramid, Castle, and La Plata, all fourteeners. And we were higher than all of it, we proudly kept telling ourselves and one another.

Paul snapped a few group photos on top, and then it was time for the gravy. Skiing backcountry corn is so radically different from the ski area version that it might as well be another sport. You put your body in the same positions, but that's where the similarities end. The snow, shaped only by sun, wind, and gravity, is uniform and dense, but porous and grippy, an endless, tilted topography of crushed velvet. If you time it right, you descend in the interval between ice and mush, carving hundreds of effortless arcs in an inch or two of melted surface snow that bubbles your edges like shore break foam, spraying and swishing out into gravity. There is virtually no avalanche danger, it's warm, you earned every turn yourself, there are no hidden obstacles, and if this kind of thing doesn't make you smile, try another planet.

Lou is one of the preeminent American ski mountaineers, and his ski technique reflects years of extreme backcountry descents from summits like the Maroon Bells, Crestone Needle, and Pyramid Peak—places where mistakes are not an option. Each turn reminded me of a Swiss watch. His contact with the snow was smooth, carved, consistent.

Zack was teaching boarding in the Crested Butte Ski School. As he got the feel for the ride, his turns got faster and fatter and more confident: deep, round arcs. He got that grin all skiers and boarders get when gravity, snow, and grace come together in a way too exuberant to keep secret.

We spiraled down the gentle summit cone and headed for the maw of Box Creek Cirque, the gigantic east-facing hole we'd skirted to our left on the ascent. One by one, we churned down the fall line to the point where it rolled out of sight. On the last pitch of the approach, looking down, all I could see was a carpet of brilliant white with Lou's careful turns silhouetted against the lake at the base of the cirque a thousand feet below.

We were half an hour later than we should have been, and the first few turns on the face had to go in snow that had become too soft. This was dangerous. If any of us broke through and fell forward, we would arrive at the bottom sooner than doctors recommend, and after being strained through a rock band in need of orthodontia. A single board was an advantage, as the increased surface area kept Zack on top. The skiing was tricky with an older school free heel, one of the longest and most exposed pitches that steep I've ever skied on pins—but after a few turns the snow firmed up again, and most of the run was adrenalized, free-fall bliss, though I skied it parallel for the power of the platform.

We all hit the snow beach of the lake euphoric from a big line on a big mountain. Even Paul, burdened down like a camel with camera gear and on one of his first excursions in alpine touring boots, arrived with a smile.

The floor of Box Creek Cirque is at 12,800 feet, higher than the summit of almost any lift in North America—and we had plenty of skiing to go. The next 1,200 verts took us through rolling hillsides and drainages, all covered with sweet, rippled corn. A few hundred feet into the trees we finally had to dismount and bushwhack back to the trail. The hike out was hot and soggy, but when we reached the parking lot at two-thirty, Lou's wife, Lisa, arrived with a cooler of beer. We stripped ski clothes, pulled sore feet from boots, soaked up sun, camaraderie, and various liquids, and congratulated ourselves like roosters after a great barnyard scratch.

Depending on whose numbers you believe, Colorado has somewhere around 650 summits over thirteen thousand feet. Many offer multiple ski descents, yet with a small number of exceptions, there are no lifts anywhere near their summits or even on their flanks. The fact is that most of the resorts barely hoist skiers out of the valley, let alone anywhere near the biggest peaks. Yet these big peaks are not as daunting as they seem, and many, like Elbert, ascend directly from some dirt road. In a single summer's day excursion, the four of us had signed the biggest one of all, with every kind of sliding stick.

After sopapillas and tacos back in Leadville, Lou and Lisa headed home to Carbondale, and Paul down to Denver on business. The sun was setting as Zack and I shot down Highway 50 on our way back to Crested Butte. Towering above us, laced with our faint tracks, Box Creek Cirque glittered in the afternoon sunshine. Zack was glued to the window. How much fun had he had? I heard that the next week he went back to try Mt. Massive. He got thundered off, but I know why he went.

It's fun to carve a big one.

—In memoriam, Paul Gallaher, 1954 – 2012

14

Back to the Butte

After living in Crested Butte for a decade, my wife and I tried to move away. When we announced we were leaving, long-time locals nodded their heads, smiled knowingly, and said things like, "We tried that once," but Emily and I just laughed at them. Ha ha. We'd had enough—or thought we'd had enough—of first tracks in Phoenix Bowl, of small-town politics, of making pies and jam from the wild raspberries in Wolverine Basin, of mountain-biking trail 401 in shoulder-high flowers while hummingbirds fought in the sweet July air, of Impressionist sunsets, huge backcountry descents, good friends, perfect double rainbows, etc. Enough with the rainbows already.

So on July 7, 2004, I clambered up into the driver's seat of a rusting, monster U-Haul and spent four wretched days lashing it across the desert to southern California, to see what life might be like on the outside. We'd lived all over the place before settling in Crested Butte and starting a family in the early 1990s, and figured we might as well give California a shot. Something about endless sunshine, big city culture, surfing, and a good job. I can't really recall.

Even the truck didn't want to go. It kept breaking down in the 105° heat, and I remember thinking that I now understood why the government used to conduct nuclear tests in the Mojave: the before and after pictures look the same. Nuclear test? What nuclear test?

I knew I'd entered another part of the world when signs started appearing at the gas stations saying things like "Teller is armed." But I forged bravely onward, like the Joads in *The Grapes of Wrath*, lumbering west in my compromised diesel behemoth, searching for the promised land.

About thirty minutes after school let out the following spring, my wife basically packed up our children and a few books and valuables and said, "We're going to CB for the summer. See you in a few months." This struck me as a clear sign that I should consider moving back. Later that summer, after many long talks, we finally did reach that decision and put the California house on the market. I then drove our little red Subaru back across the great desert. So, probably not much wiser (though we did hire pros this time to move our furniture) but definitely a year older we returned to Crested Butte and saw it in a different light. Here with some thick description, as the anthropologists like to call it, are some thoughts about what makes the place so special, from the perspective of someone who has been there and back again.

The first thing I noticed when I got back had to do with the Subaru itself. In Orange County, driving a little Subaru feels a bit odd. People look down at you from the command posts of their sparkling yellow Hummers, or up at you as they blow past in their cute little Jaguar speedsters, furrow their brows, and then turn away as if embarrassed. Apparently my car had marked me as an Untouchable, or maybe worse, a Democrat atheist. Wait a minute . . . I *am* an Untouchable!

But that's another story. The Subaru liked being back in Crested Butte. Everyone talks about the Butte's funky old houses and the bicycles, but I don't think the internal combustion machines get their due. After all, we drive off-road. And on ice. With studs, dude. Yep, *we have pieces of metal sticking out of our tires.* Our cars have serious stories to tell.

My first evening home I was emptying out the happy little Subaru after driving back across the Mojave. Rico, the orange cat who had stayed with our house-sitters for the year, and who I'm sure didn't remember me even though I'm the one who saved his scrawny kitten butt from the pound, was rubbing against my leg in the dark. Generally a nice feeling. I'd like to think he had missed me, but he was probably just hungry. I was sporting shorts and flip-flops and, holding a pile of stuff in my arms, I gracefully closed the Subaru door with a hip check. Although it was dark, I could tell from the immediate howling, hissing, and snarling that something had gone horribly wrong, and you'd probably make sounds like that too if you were hanging by your tail from a car door. Even a Subaru. Humanitarian that I am I immediately opened the door. Well, I tried to open the door, but it was locked, and as I fished for the keys Rico went after my leg like a fresh piece of fish, or a mouse whose time has come.

What does this have to do with Crested Butte? Well, I wound up in the hospital the next day with a colony of *Pasteurella Multocida*, a bacteria common in the mouths of cats that does particularly unpleasant things when injected into a human leg. This particular colony was trying to eat me for lunch. Upon seeing this, the kind people at the Gunnison Valley Hospital put enough IV antibiotics into my body to kill every microbe within twenty feet. I was there for two days and doctor after doctor, nurse after nurse whom I had come to know over the years—people who had worked for me at one place or another, or delivered our children, or with whom we had gone cross-country skiing under a full moon, or traveled with us to the South Pacific—would walk in and say "Dave! Great to see you!" which struck me as a bit odd under the circumstances, as I was unshaven, smelly, infected, drooling, and occasionally whimpering with fear that they were going to cut off my leg. But it was a touching gesture nonetheless.

That kind of thing just doesn't happen in most other places. On the one hand, it can be a bit odd when the woman who was your son's nanny and is now training to be a nurse is changing your IV, but it's sort of reassuring as well. I knew who she was and I trusted her and honestly, that made it hurt less. Well, sort of.

So I'd been in town for two days and already I owed deep thanks and maybe even my life, to Lee Lynch, Colleen O'Sullivan, Laurie Garren, Jay McMurren, Barb Hammond, Ariel Tidwell, Abby Kunes, Christine Holbrook, Shannon and many others. Thanks, guys.

And the leg is ok. Cool scar, too. And I didn't break Rico's tail.

That was when it struck me that this sense of community—so often invoked but rarely described in its gritty reality—is ultimately what Crested Butte and a few other great mountain towns are all about. The lifts and the backcountry offer up great skiing, but the town is more unusual than the mountains. The sense of community extends further, and is more subtle than most realize. If you're a visitor, you may notice after a while, that locals do something that the Telluride writer Peter Shelton has called "the wave." He doesn't mean thousands of people standing up in a stadium and spilling beer all over each other, but the way that people greet each other when just passing by all day long. Slight raising of the eyebrows, one hand off the steering wheel or the bike handlebars, nod of the head, smile. OK, it happens in Telluride too, but CB waves are better.

It's hard to figure out what the wave signifies, because it's more than "Hello," but somehow different than "How are you?" In my view it's something along the lines of "Howdy," which is of course just the first half of "How do you do?" Howdy. Everything's ok here, just lettin' ya know. Nice to see ya. Hope you're good. On we go . . .

People don't do the wave on major freeways. Nor do they do it on the streets of developments, nope, just don't do it. It can get sort of lonesome without the wave. But it is after all impractical when traveling eighty miles an hour on a sixteen-laner, or trying to cross Madison Ave. at 54th Street. Dangerous, even. Frankly, attempting to be that familiar is just a bit suspicious to most folks in such circumstances. As the Irish like to say in New York, "Laugh and the world laughs with you . . . but not on the IRT." No, they move away, hold their belongings just a wee bit tighter to their chests and readjust their iPods. Try it sometime. You'll see. It took me a while to get out of the habit of the wave when we left town. In Los Angeles, people usually seemed to think it was preparation for a drive-by shooting. It was a pleasure to be back doing it again. Sometimes I would go out and walk around just to do gratuitous waves. Hey, how are 'ye.

Community matters in Crested Butte on a larger scale, too. Of course, it can be embarrassing when the people who run the local flower stores remember the dates of important events in your life better than you do but it all generally sorts itself out because they're always willing to work with you as a team.

True story:

Ring. "Hello?"

"Hi Dave, it's Linda, over at the florists. Isn't it your anniversary today? Need some flowers?"

"Uh, wait a . . . yes, uh, of course, er . . . I was just going to . . . how about a dozen roses?

"Great! Where should I deliver them?"

This kind of thing applies to raising children as well. People are always looking out for your kid, even if there's a certain lack of privacy. A conversation may begin in the produce section of the supermarket with a question like, "So, is little Johnny still a dyslexic bed wetter? Getting a bit old for that isn't he . . . hey, I read this great book . . . " Honestly, you might reply, I just want to buy some lettuce. But I have to say I prefer that whole thing to the situation some other places I have lived where people seem to have a rather astonishing level of fear about the world.

Cue the soccer field. *Thwop thwop thwop thwop . . .*

"Coach, this is Mrs. Jones. Johnny's a bit late for practice, so I have him incoming to the LZ at the southwest corner of the field on his dad's Cobra attack helicopter. He'll be attending practice today with his SAT tutor. . . ."

"Roger that, Mrs. Jones, LZ clear, proceed, we have shin guards and #2 pencils . . . "

Spend a little too much time around that kind of thing and you can start to doubt yourself. You catch yourself thinking, life *is* sort of dangerous, and, you know, maybe I *do* need a Cobra attack helicopter. And of course, that's a slippery slope, because after the Cobra attack helicopter come the Botox parties and the shiny little lime-green shoes and then you need a nicer place to park the stupid helicopter and it just goes on and on.

In most of these places, people don't even think about going somewhere on a bicycle, whereas in Crested Butte children have the run of the entire town on one by the time they're ten.

Another true story: when we were moving into our new home beyond the great desert, one day the neighbor across the street saw me on my bicycle and said "Oh—that's *your* bicycle."

Of course I said *Yes* and looked a bit puzzled. By way of explanation she then said that she hadn't thought we were "bicycle people." By which, I suddenly realized, she meant poor and / or brown. She was a very nice person, actually, but, I thought, she just comes from a different place . . . but then I realized, suddenly, that I was the one from a different place. Oops.

I wanted to tell her that in the town where I used to live, things are different. People go to work on their bicycles. They go out to dinner on their bicycles. They climb mountains on their bicycles. They ride them in January (that stud thing again). They light them on fire and jump through hoops on Elk Avenue. Well, some of them do. I wanted to say, it's a bit like Holland, just higher. And I love bicycle people.

But I didn't say any of that. I just smiled and said something like "Yeah, this is my bicycle."

We had a great year in California, though it was in fact cold and damp, just as the song says. Second or third wettest year on record. The skiing in the San Gabriels, right above L.A., was excellent, or "sick bird," as CB locals sometimes say. Bomber maritime snowpack, lifts running into May at Mt. Baldy. We started to make friends, but like everyone in the L.A. area, realized that our friends were scattered like grapeshot all over the place. We went to the amazing beaches. I bought a surfboard and had a lot of fun being thrown repeatedly on my face. We went to the concerts, we ate at the fancy restaurants, we went shopping for Cobra attack helicopters, we learned how to enter the freeway like a bullet and pass on the right at high speed, punching it through the blind spot.

But in the end, we missed our friends. We missed the wave. We missed being bicycle people. We missed going to the hospital, or the post office, or the flower store, or the grocery store and hearing the latest news, even if it was about us and totally untrue.

And yes, we missed the rainbows, the big double fatties, every color clear and sparkling, arcing over the Butte late summer afternoons when a thunderstorm is lifting off and the entire valley seems to be taking stock of itself and saying "Oooh, I am so beautiful, no Botox for me, thank you very much, just watch this . . . "

And so we moved back to the land where snow first drapes the high peaks in late September, then turns into a dangerously faceted continental snowpack by Christmas; where everyone seems to know your business and yet you all feel dwarfed by the larger business of mountains; where my sons can bike to school and I can bike to work and my wife and I can ride our bikes when we go out to dinner; and where life goes on in the way of post-industrial villages, connected to the world by jets, cables, repeaters, satellites and automobiles, but the day-to-day remains human.

That humanity is the real reason why people visit not just mountains, but also mountain towns, and become enchanted or fall in love with the place to the point that they can't leave. Those of us who have lived there were drawn in not only by the perfect beauty, but also by the flawed humanity. The mountains and the town exist in a balance that is more and more rare. "In wildness lies the preservation of the world"—Thoreau didn't say wildness *was* the world, he said its preservation lies there—but that world includes us and how we live as well. That's the town.

At any rate, it was good to be back, even if we didn't stay. We now live most of the year in Boulder, which is almost a mountain town, and we still spend at least three months a year in Crested Butte. After all, it's a big world out there, and it's good to explore. And moving far away taught me something: how hard it is to leave, and why so many people have tried and failed. It's always good to come back to the Butte.

Part Two

Making Sure It Goes On

15

Making Sure It Goes On

Skiing is an individual activity, but a social sport. Even ski races, measured against the lonely clock, can take place only with a crowd. And when you stand utterly alone on a peak, every step and turn you make has a technical history; every piece of gear and its development has a history; unless you are making a first descent, the mountain you are on has a ski history; and you have a history filled with interactions with thousands of other people, those who ski and those who don't. Every step you take and each turn you make is haunted by the sweat, joy, triumphs, challenges and defeat of people you know and people you don't.

It's easy to forget this, but sometimes we're given the opportunity to see it unfold before our eyes.

The year my older son, Jacob, was eleven, he was racing as a first-year J IV. That's a hard year, as the second-year IVs, who are twelve, are bigger and stronger, sometimes a lot bigger and stronger. Jake made good progress, although he didn't qualify for the Junior Olympics. This meant that he was invited to Colorado's consolation race, the Council Cup, held each year in March at Ski

Cooper, near Leadville. One boy and one girl from this series (one super-G, two GSs and two slaloms) advance to the JOs. Everybody else simply has a good time and thinks about next year.

I'm the former ski racer in the family, and I looked forward to spending a long weekend with my boy. We'd been taking road trips since he was five or six. As I now do with my younger son, Noah, we tell jokes, eat Mexican food, go skiing, crash in bad hotels.

Being a parent at a ski race is a bit like being a sherpa. You spend the day ferrying clothes and skis and food up and down the hill. I make this more interesting by strapping on my skins and climbing through the spectator alley, stopping to watch, to talk to friends and coaches, to get a feel for the scene.

Climbing Ski Cooper has historical resonance. It was here and in the surrounding mountains that the 10th Mountain Division trained in the early 1940s before shipping out to Europe to fight in some of the fiercest battles of WWII. Clambering around on the gentle, uncrowded hill is great exercise and connects you to a crucial piece of ski history, as it was the gallant boys of the 10th who came home to start many of the greatest ski areas in America.

The last day of the race was slalom day. In the base lodge, I noticed there was a buffet table set up and a lot of older guys—quite a bit older—suiting up and greeting each other with handshakes, hugs, and slaps on the back. I asked around and learned that it was the annual reunion for remaining members of the 10th. The room was filled with people who should qualify as American heroes in anyone's book—all of them at least eighty years old, many heading out for a day of turns.

In between his races, at lunch, I dragged Jacob over to meet some of them. He couldn't understand what all the fuss was about. He told the vets his name and one of them said "Well, we had a good friend named Jacob. He trained with us, but you know, he didn't come back from Europe." My Jacob said, "Oh," and there was a

silence. Then they turned back to each other and started talking
again about their lives. I would have loved to stay, but they were
there to talk to each other, after all, not some pesky racer dad. And
it was almost inspection time and we only had a few minutes to
grab a bite.

While we were eating our French fries, some of the racers sat
down at a table next to ours where one of the vets was taking
a break.

"You boys racing today?" he asked.

Boys, cautiously addressing someone seventy years older: "Yeah."

"What is it today?"

"Slalom."

"You having fun?"

Mouths full of hamburger: "Mm-hmm."

Pause. Then the vet leaned over and said, "Is it fast?" He smiled.

The boys nodded and kept eating. Who was this old guy, anyway?

After lunch, while my son was inspecting his second course, I
saw a parade of skiers making their way down the front of the
mountain. It was the vets. Out in front one was skiing without
poles, carrying a large American flag that was snapping crisply in
what had turned into a blustery day.

"That's John Woodward," somebody said. "He's the senior guy
here, so he carries the flag."

I've done a bit of research since that time. Woodward was born
in 1915. In college at the University of Washington in the 1930s,
he was captain of the ski team. In 1936, he took fifth at the U.S.
Olympic ski trials and was an alternate for the U.S. team. He raced
in the very first Harriman Cup ski races at Sun Valley in the mid-
1930s. After joining the 3rd Division's 15th Regiment at Fort Lewis,
Washington, in 1940, he led a series of lengthy patrols in the area
of Mt. Rainer. On May 12, 1943, already a Captain, he became
Commander of the 10th Cavalry Reconnaissance Group ("The 10th

Recon"), which later merged into the 87th. This was the group of crack mountaineers who trained many of the others in the 10th. He rose to the rank of Major, saw extensive action in Italy, and was later involved in the ski industry.[1]

Last I heard, John Woodward still races. He's the oldest active ski racer in America, perhaps in the world. About three weeks after that day in 2006 at Cooper, he was the only entrant and therefore the victor in Class 14 (90+) at the USSA Masters National Championships at Sunday River, in Maine. Remember, this man probably competed in his first ski race *in the 1920s*. And I can tell you he still knows how to make a good turn while carrying a large flag in a stiff breeze. He was still active in 2011, at the age of ninety-six.

At the bottom of his run at Cooper, I went up to Woodward and asked him if I could take his picture. I think he's used to the request. He pulled up his goggles and flashed me a big smile.

Everyone in America who is a skier owes these men and their families a great debt, not only for their service to their country, but also for their role in creating modern American skiing. Many tend to think of that only in terms of the ski areas they built, but it also has everything to do with the gear, and the turns, and the mountaineering. Every man in the 10th was a ski mountaineer. That was the whole point. There were no lifts on Riva Ridge. When they started skiing, you climbed for every turn. Our sport simply would not look the same without what they accomplished throughout their lives, both in peace and through unfortunate necessity in battle.

I stowed my camera, thanked Major Woodward, put my pack on my back and began climbing. One thousand feet above me, Jacob was preparing for what would be the best slalom run he's ever had. I remember thinking that there was almost a hundred years of living ski and ski mountaineering generations on that mountain

---

1   Many thanks to Peter Shelton and Lou Dawson for this background.

at that moment, including not only Woodward, my son, and me, but hundreds of others: Tenth Mountain vets and their families, Council Cup racers and their families, other skiers and patrollers and staff and teachers and students and more.

To be part of such a community, all of us enjoying the day, connected to so many others in this most individual of sports—that's quite a privilege.

Our time in the mountains is ephemeral. It is more delicate than the words that describe it, for even the most beautiful turns vanish like smoke, never to return. And yet each step we take has a past, a history that includes not only our own lives, but the lives and the work—and the sacrifice—of many others. Each step we take in the mountains is like finding a message in a bottle. May we all take many more.

And then, reader, whoever you may be: pass it on.

JOHN WOODWARD WITH HIS WIFE VERONE WOODWARD ON MOUNT BALDY NEAR SUN VALLEY, IDAHO. APRIL, 1942. COURTESY OF THE DENVER PUBLIC LIBRARY WESTERN COLLECTION.

JOHN B. WOODWARD (FOREGROUND) AND PETER GABRIEL (BACKGROUND) PRACTICE
ICE CLIMBING TECHNIQUES ON NISQUALLI GLACIER, MT. RAINIER, WASHINGTON.
JUNE 1942.

JOHN WOODWARD MAKING SURE IT GOES ON AT
SKI COOPER, MARCH 2006.
PHOTO BY DAVID J. ROTHMAN.

JACOB ROTHMAN MAKING SURE IT GOES ON AT SKI COOPER, MARCH 2008.
PHOTO BY SKI PIX.COM.

16

Bridget Goes to Monarch

So I'm standing in my long johns at dusk one April afternoon in the parking lot at the top of Monarch Pass. The lightweight red ones, my favorites. I'm on my way from Crested Butte to Denver and it's a long drive. I always stop at the pass if I have time and do a little tour. Twenty-minute climb to the Continental Divide, ski a power line with no starting zone and a good pitch for close to one thousand feet, skins back on, up to the car. Total time usually about an hour, then back onto the road. The low point on the tour is about eleven thousand feet—the snow can be splendid. This day, however, it's been pretty weak—refreezing mank, a bit tricky with a free heel, threatening to toss me without warning on my face all the way down. But it's all good.

A car drifts through the parking lot, a Subaru wagon, then makes a circle and slows down right next to me. I wonder if I'm going to get yelled at for changing my pants in a public place, but there's nobody here but us. The window comes down to reveal a young woman with a worried look. Blonde ponytail. Slight coffee stain on her pale wool zip-up sweater. Leaning over across the passenger seat as I approach.

"Do you know where the nearest gas station is?"

"Where you headed?"

"That way." She points east, my direction as well, wipes away a tear. This is odd.

"Sure—there's one in Poncha, at the bottom of the pass . . . "

"Are you, oh, this is terrible, but . . . do you have forty dollars so I can buy some gas? I—I'm lost and—I have to get back to Fort Collins tonight. And I'm out of cash and didn't realize it was so far. . . . "

Now this is an interesting situation. I'm standing at dusk in my skivvies, surrounded by discarded telemark gear, talking to a beautiful young woman in a parking lot at more than eleven thousand feet. How can you be lost here? *There's only one road . . .* and you're astride a geological feature visible from the moon. But I suppose we forget what the mountains are like for people who don't spend much time in them.

It does occur to me that she might be yanking my chain—let's see, can I get this random man to give me forty dollars? I think I can, I think I can . . .

"Here," she says tearfully and offers a small yellow pad with a pen, "Write down your address and I'll send you the money when I get home, I promise."

I go back to my car, dig out forty, and give it to her. Write down my address. Tell her how to find the gas station and go back to changing as she drives off east.

Fifteen minutes later I'm at the bottom of the pass and there she is, at the closed gas station. I pull in. She waves sheepishly.

"You look so different—" she says as I get out.

"—with my clothes on?" Come on, who could resist that? She giggles. I pull a credit card—she doesn't have one—and activate the pump. As the gas kicks in, she tells me she's studying to be a CPA, that her name is Bridget. Then when she's done, slightly confused—she hands me the receipt. I'd laugh but that wouldn't be very nice. Says that she's driven her friend all the way back up to Crested Butte, where she teaches at Stepping Stones Day Care, and hadn't realized how far it was. I consider giving a lecture about the mountains, about planning, making a wisecrack about what it takes to be a CPA, that she should keep the receipt to remember how much she spent and send it to me with the check. But I refrain.

She tries to give me back the forty, but I only take twenty. I can just see the headlines . . ." Young Thing Starves on Drive Home to Fort Collins; Cheapskate Telemark Dirtbag Journalist Held Without Bail." She drives off.

We meet yet again as we buy the incredibly bad coffee at the Gunsmoke Truck Stop near Buena Vista, where 285 turns toward Denver. When I come up to the counter, there are five or six dollars sitting on top.

"She left that for you," says the good ol' boy running the register, eyeing me suspiciously.

I thank him, nod, pocket the change, and head out. Bridget is nowhere in sight. The Subaru is gone. It's pitch dark and I imagine her on her way home. An hour later, I think I pass her coming down off Kenosha Pass into Bailey, but I'm not sure. I roll down the window and wave anyways. Haven't heard from her since.

And so it goes—America's a great country. I bet this kind of thing doesn't happen everywhere. And I bet it doesn't happen on golf courses, either. But in the world of telemark skiing and back-country camaraderie, it doesn't seem out of place. It's one of the reasons I do it. I like the people. Although I don't think Bridget was a telemark skier. So I guess it goes a bit further than that. I even like who I am when I'm telemarking. If I'd been a snowmobiler, who knows what I might have done? Probably demanded collateral.

Easy guys, I'm just kidding.

So Bridget, if you read this—please bring a credit card, warm clothes and a map the next time you venture forth. Crested Butte is a long way from . . . well, almost everything. And try telemarking. It's a big country out there, and it gets cold. Free-heel skis can be useful if you need to go for help. And send me that check if you feel like it, but if you can't or if you forget, or if you've lost my address—don't worry about it.

You've already given me something else.

17

To an Athlete Dying Young

Smart lad, to slip betimes away
From fields where glory does not stay,
And early though the laurel grows
It withers quicker than the rose.
—A. E. Housman

He had the perfect name: Asher Crank. How could you possibly grow up with that name in a ski town and not learn how to rip?

And learn he did. His mother, Stephanie Watkins, owned one of the best ski shops in town and he was on the hill all the time. While still a J IV ski racer, he was already in the first couple of seeds of the Rocky-Central Division for his age group and climbing the ladder. Then in ninth grade, he quit racing to focus on big mountain skiing and freeriding. His alpine coaches, sorry to lose such obvious talent, tried to get him to run gates for a few more years, but he was determined.

Asher loved new school skiing. By the time he was sixteen, he was already comfortable with trips to regional and national podiums in halfpipe, slopestyle, skiercross and big mountain events. He must have ranked in the first seed of up-and-coming junior American free skiers. He was good and he was ready.

I'm not sure when I first met Asher. He was always there, spending time in his folks' shop, running gates, running around. I knew Crested Butte Academy could serve him well and I remember how pleased everyone at the school was when he joined us. I was looking forward to having him in the halls. After all, the word "Asher" in Hebrew means "happy" or "blessed," and Asher lived up to that name. Even when he was in trouble—a regular event—and trying to avoid the staff, Asher was a little bit like a sneaky ray of sunshine. He had a big smile and wasn't afraid to use it.

That charm came in handy at times. Asher didn't have any adult men fully in his life. His family situation was complicated. That may have had something to do with why he was a bit wild. During Asher's last year of alpine racing, when he was in eighth grade, the team went down to Telluride for a race. Despite careful protocols to make sure students were never unsupervised, somehow three of them, Asher, Didrik, and Josh, wound up in a condo for a few hours on their own. Borat and the guys who make the Jackass movies would have been impressed, perhaps even awed, with what ensued. Imagine what two thirteen-year-old boys might conceive of as the absolutely most disgusting thing to do with a blender when their friend is in the shower. And they might have gotten away with it all, except that Asher and Didrik didn't count on the fact that Josh wouldn't stay in the shower after they had thrown an excrement smoothie on him, but would come out and chase them around the condo, doing about ten thousand dollars' worth of damage in thirty seconds.

When Brian Krill, my director of Athletic Education, called me at seven a.m. the next day, the first thing he said was, "Are you sitting down?" Such is the life of a headmaster.

When the team returned and we were drawing together our judicial committee at the school to deal with what the boys had wrought, I remember each member of the committee, as I explained to him or her what had happened, looking at me incredulously and saying, "They did what?!" Yes, I would say, that's what they did. Yes, they did. And you can't laugh during the meeting. This is serious. We might get sued. For a lot. And then we would talk about exactly how to address it. You should have heard the phone calls to the parents. It was a memorable day.

There were apologies, there were tears, there was contrition and some gnashing of teeth. At a certain point, when the pale light of moral reasoning began to shine through, Asher looked at me, on the edge of tears, half-sobbing, and finally admitted, "Well, I . . . I guess . . . it wasn't . . . a very good idea." There were suspensions, checks had to be written and there was a lot of work the following summer. But in the end what I and everyone else saw was that these were three wonderful boys and we were glad they were in our school. They were going to be fine. And indeed it all worked itself out and the boys remained at the school and remained fast friends. Didrik and Josh graduated and went on to college and are probably done by now. The third was of course Asher. I have looked forward already for years to telling them all how funny the whole thing really was.

After l'affaire Telluride, Asher worked hard to fly under my radar, and he was good at it. He understood stealth. But I had my own stealthy ways and I was always watching him because he was a leader in his class and a lovely kid. You could feel his exuberant energy from around a corner. He was also one of the most handsome boys in the school. I would see girls look at him as he passed by and say, "Hi, Asher . . ." in a tone that is impossible to convey in print, a mix of affection, longing, and desire that I know I have never, ever experienced in my entire life. Asher would smile, say something like, "Hey . . . how are 'ye?" and keep on strolling. A truly charismatic boy. One of the local restaurants, The Last Steep, named a dish after him, the Asher Crank Salad Caesar, "A traditional style Caesar salad topped with a scoop of Caribbean crawfish salad," which was something he'd thought up. Why "Salad Caesar" instead of "Caesar Salad" I don't know.

After I had left the Academy and was living in California for a year, he probably thought I wasn't paying attention, but of course I followed his results as he started to shine in his chosen sport. When I returned to town, he had magically grown a foot and the resentment seemed to have evaporated. Instead of averting his gaze whenever he saw me, he smiled, looked me in the eye and said "Hey Dave!" Shook my hand. Told me about his results, about school. I always looked forward to that. One time I saw him riding a rail from the chair and he made it look as easy as water flowing downhill. That fall I'd heard that he was (finally!) passing his classes, and I knew he was stomping his competitions. He was talking about going to college. Asher was going to be fine, just fine. I was looking forward to his graduation in 2007.

Then, on Saturday, January 13 of that year, Asher was with his team preparing for a slope-style event at Copper. On a training run, with coaches and teammates watching, he came blazing into the biggest hit in the park, riding switch. He went big, his timing was off, and though he landed on his feet something went wrong and he was thrown immediately onto his head. Ben Somrak, one of Asher's coaches and an EMT, was on the scene within seconds and says it was clear from the first moment just how dangerous the injury was. According to him, Asher's pupils were already dilated, sure sign of a serious head injury. He was unresponsive, bleeding, and soon went into convulsions. On the flight-for-life to Denver he went into cardiac arrest and was resuscitated but never regained consciousness. The next day, after heroic efforts by his doctors, it became clear that he was never coming back and his family made the excruciating decision to let him go. I remember where I was when I heard the news, but the rest of the day is gone.

My wife and I were in Boulder that weekend, and when we drove over and asked if we could leave a note for the family, the attendant at the other end of the line said, with a sigh and an apology, that since we had last called—a mere forty-five minutes—Asher was no longer a patient. It was one of the most sorrowful sentences I have ever heard.

The next weekend most of the town turned out for Asher's memorial, but I and many of his coaches couldn't attend, as there was a JIII-IV Super-G in Durango (my own son was in the race). The coaches had decided that Asher would have wanted everyone to go, so the race was on.

The night before his memorial, I visited the coaches in their condo, where they were tuning skis. We've all known each other for years. The conversation turned to Asher and every one had a story. Steve Hamilton told of the time that Asher and some friends snuck off to ski a forbidden chute with mandatory air on Crested Butte's North Face. They were about twelve, and Steve looked up from the bottom to see them literally dangling from rocks and branches and had to hand out consequences. Others told stories of Asher leaving his race skis at the top of the course at the end of the day; of showing up late for training and having to hike up the hill as penance. Story after story—laughter and tears. I think it was Steve who summed it up at one point. After a pause in the conversation he said, "Asher was the kind of kid who woke up every day without knowing what he was necessarily going to do—and then he just went out and had a great time."

Crested Butte is small, and there were times when the Academy and the Ski Club, the two racing organizations in those days, didn't always get along. In retrospect, one of the memorable things about that evening in Durango was that in the room were three coaches or teachers who had worked with Asher at the Academy—Brian Krill, Dolly Schaub (both of whom were then coaching for the Club), and me—and three others who had worked with Asher at the Club—Steve Hamilton, Marnie Joslyn, and Dolly's husband Reed Schaub. As the anecdotes went around the room, I now realize, it was Asher who was helping us to remember what we should always keep in mind—it's all about the kids, and they are more precious than any of us can really say. What a cliché: every day matters. Perhaps part of Asher's legacy was to help to draw us all together in that way. I'd like to think so.

Although it hurts, I owe Asher a debt for reminding me of what a privilege it is to have been part of his life and to have been one of his teachers. It was an honor to serve him and through him everyone in his family, even when he trashed a condo with excrement. In fact, especially then, because it was at that moment that I fully gained his trust by not expelling him, as some of the teachers, understandably enraged, felt we should have. But the boys were young. It was the coaches who were not supposed to have left them alone. And while it took a while to kick in, those boys were sincerely contrite. Rules are only as good as the judgments which execute them, and in this case, expulsion would have been wrong. After all, Telluride has plenty of condos, but there was only one Asher. And that will never, ever be over. I can take that knowledge with me to the very next time I ever work with any student, anywhere. I am grateful to him for teaching me what it means to be a teacher, how incredibly important it is to choose carefully in a crisis.

Grizzled old Zen headmaster to rookie: "Where do good decisions come from, grasshopper?"

"I do not know, sir."

"Experience."

"Ah—"

"And where does experience come from?"

"The infinite vortex of reality?"

"No, you idiot. Experience comes from bad decisions. . . ."

And I have plenty of . . . experience. In Asher's case, however, I know I made a good decision and that as a result we both reaped a reward, albeit a terribly brief one. Asher's untimely death gave permanent gravitas to the observation that good teachers teach their subjects, but those who aspire to be great ones must also teach their students. Which is harder than it sounds, especially when you confront a blender full of boy poo spattered on drapes.

Skiing is beautiful but can be dangerous. If anyone knew what he was doing, however, it was Asher. He was talented, experienced and skilled. He just landed wrong. And amidst all the grief, I'd like to think that his final thoughts were joyful ones:

"Man, I'm going big. It is so cool up here. Every day's a new day. Oh, I love skiing, I love life, and I'm free."

18

Send In the Clowns

Sometime in the fall of 2005 I was soaking my bones in the hot tub at the Crested Butte Club when Nick Rayder came in to soak his as well. We got to talking about this and that.

I don't remember when I first met Nick. In Crested Butte you run into the same people so often that sometimes it's hard to recall when the understanding of another person began to coalesce. It happens in hundreds of little daily encounters, at the post office, on the hill, on the trails, through work and play and politics. Nick was always around, at fund-raisers, at events, supporting good causes. He would show up at benefits for the Crested Butte Music Festival, which I had co-founded, and donate generously. He gave a large collection of old sheet music to Crested Butte Academy. After Emily and I returned from our misadventures on the alien traffic planet of Southern California, he bought some of our extra furniture. I would see his skillfully executed drawings and paintings here and there. He was always a clown in the Fourth of July parade, and always seemed to be enjoying himself. I remember a long talk we had at the Paradise Café as I stumbled around in the depths of a mid-life crisis. He seemed to understand exactly what I was going through, though I wasn't sure why at the time. And at some point I realized he was an unusual man.

Nick's slowly advancing multiple sclerosis is one of the reasons he's been spending more and more time during the winters in Scottsdale, where the climate is easier. This I'd known for a while, but that day at the club, I could see that it was getting harder for him to move around. So, in the course of our chat that afternoon in the tub, when he asked me if I would be a clown with him in the Fourth of July parade the following summer, I agreed. I figured I'd help him out.

After I had made the offer, I thought, why did I do that? I love Nick, but I don't like parades much, even though Crested Butte's is special. It is pure Americana, democratic to the edge of anarchy. Floats feature everything from businesses to politicians to religious groups to environmental organizations to a bunch of guys drinking beer on a flatbed truck, people walking their dogs, a big water fight at the end, you name it. But it's noisy and chaotic and my children used to cry when they were little. Also, if I'm around that many people, I worry that someone might announce we've all just been drafted or perhaps that we should storm the jail, and it spooks me. I don't think I've ever actually participated in a parade in my life. I switched from clarinet to bassoon in junior high so I wouldn't have to march in parades. Let alone dressed up as a clown. What would I know about clowning? I'm an educator.

I tried throughout winter to forget what I'd promised I would do with Nick when July came around. I hoped my memory and conscience would malfunction and release me from that commitment. You know how it works . . . just ignore your obligations and maybe they'll go away.

No dice. Nick had done too many kind and generous things for me to back out. So when he called a few days before the parade I told him I'd be by the morning of the fourth. He told me he was glad because otherwise he might not have done it at all—it was getting too hard to do it on his own.

When the day came I asked my son Jacob, then twelve, if he wanted to come along. He seemed interested and off we went. On a whim I dropped by Karole Armitage's home on the way over to Nick's. When not gallivanting across the planet choreographing brilliant ballets for her own New York-based company, Armitage-Gone! and the likes of Alvin Ailey, Karole likes to spend as much time in Crested Butte as possible. Her father, Ken, was for many years a researcher at the Rocky Mountain Biological Laboratory in nearby Gothic, and is the world's leading expert on marmots, which is why Karole spent her childhood summers in the valley. Did you know that marmots are the largest animals that fully hibernate? Their heartbeats go as low as six beats per minute, they take several days to wake up, and during that time you can toss them back and forth like a basketball. Further, they . . . well that's another story.

Karole joined up with us and we arrived at Nick's about an hour before the parade. All around town the energy was climbing like local real estate values in those days—cars were parked everywhere, floats were being assembled, the usual suspects were already drunk. Nick opened his shed, pulled out the costumes and make-up kit, and we were all suddenly grateful that Karole was along, as in the course of her dance career she's probably put on makeup more times than I've eaten lunch. I, on the other hand, never progressed beyond finger-painting. Karole is highly professional and is constitutionally unable to resist a challenging deadline, so she got to work making all of us look like we worked for Barnum & Bailey. Meanwhile Nick dug around in his shed and produced enormous red bow ties and cummerbunds, white gloves, bags stuffed with candy, fright wigs, and funky top hats.

We were ready to go in a trice, which was great, because we

were riding tricycles. Well, Nick was on a motor scooter and Jacob and I were riding bicycles, but I can't say we were ready to go in a "bice," whatever that is, now can I? And so Karole headed off and the three of us rolled our way around to find our spot in the parade. We gathered on the stretch of Elk Avenue to the east of the four-way stop, and soon, with a whoop, a holler and a clanking of gears, the juggernaut got under way and we progressed up the boulevard. I didn't have the slightest idea what I was supposed to do except throw candy at children and never say a word, as Nick had instructed us is the code of the clown.

Then a funny thing happened. First off, I didn't much care for the teenagers. "Yo, check out the clown! Clown dude, like, throw me some candy or whatever!"

Not a chance.

But the littler ones—the ones between three and maybe seven or so—responded differently. They were a bit scared, a bit unsure, a bit intrigued. What was this person, if person he was? He was the same size and general shape as an adult, but there was something wrong . . . And I didn't want them to be scared, I wanted them to have fun. So, in a kind of clumsy desperation, I started falling off my little bike in front of four-year-olds as if I had just expired, which would make them laugh with glee. Then I would get up, silently wag a finger pretending to reprimand my bike for falling over, then jump back on it and ride frantically in little circles. Then I would run up to a small person and hand out lollipops, often accepted only tentatively, with a most serious and penetrating gaze.

My routine evolved as I moved up Elk, accruing flourishes, twirls, expressions, and emotions from mock hysteria to mock misery to mock hilarity. It was like a kind of music wherein all the noise and even most of the adults—including, apparently, me—had vanished and there remained the purest kind of purposeless play imaginable. No identity, only a role and a job. In the heart of all that chaos, time almost stopped—as it always does in the presence of art—and there was merely the clown and a child or two at a time in a strange little comedy whose climax was the presentation of a gift.

We gathered up by the old Town Hall at Second Street, turning south. The roar of the greasepaint was running into my eyes. Jake looked happy. Nick was tired but quietly joyous. He considered me carefully, smiled, and said "It looks like you just discovered your inner clown." Then he thanked me and Jacob for helping him out.

I think that's when it hit me, in a realization I savored all afternoon, through lunch and beer, the obligatory thunderstorm, the parties and conversations, a typically sweet Crested Butte afternoon fading into a high alpine valley evening.

I had thought I was the one doing Nick a favor. How could I have misunderstood things so completely? And that clown—he'd known this all along. Now I owe him even more.

The only question that remains is: Harlequin, Pierrot, or Auguste? Hobo or tramp? Wise fool or idiot savant? Commedia dell'arte, vaudeville, pantomime, or Hollywood? Juggler, leper, devil, or congressman? Larry, Moe, Curly, Laurel, Hardy, Groucho, Chico, Harpo, Abbott, Costello, Bert, Ernie, Bozo, Ann Coulter, or Ronald McDonald?

Whatever it may be, I say bring us our scepters and the chariot drawn by mice! Print a menu and a new license to subvert. Lay out our gloves. Let there be clowns.

Nick, I'll see you on the Fourth.

19

Nick Rayder, Mountain Town Clown

Nick Rayder has had a fascinating life. He was born in 1940, in Plainfield, New Jersey. Always bright, he was the class clown and as a result, flunked out of high school. At graduation he sat crying in the audience as his friends crossed the stage to receive their diplomas. His family had seen the writing on the wall and decided a few years earlier he would need a skill. So they sent him to the Bowery Barber College in New York City, which he attended every day in the summer after his sophomore year. Nick says the education he received was not perhaps quite what his parents had intended. The first thing the teachers taught him was how to hold a razor if he got into a fight.

As he studied how to give haircuts and shaves, Nick became interested in psychology. Every day he would see men who once had been successful but somehow wound up in the Bowery as derelicts. He got to know them because even though most couldn't afford to pay the twenty-five cents for a haircut, on slow days when the students needed to practice giving shaves they'd haul these guys in off the street.

After high school, Nick was accepted on probation at Lycoming College on the basis of his earlier grades (they didn't know he'd flunked out). He earned a diploma in summer school, matriculated in 1959, and proceeded "to learn how to learn" as he puts it, discovering he was a strong student. He majored in psychology, then decided to attend graduate school in Colorado "to see the mountains." He earned a Master's in Industrial Psychology at Colorado State University on a research assistantship. Then, in 1965, he joined the military because his academic mentor at the time said "he needed to grow up." He was accepted to the San Diego Naval Research Laboratory with a commission as a Naval Officer in Research and Evaluation, and even enrolled . . . but at the last minute decided not to go. Instead, he headed off to the University of Northern Colorado at Greeley for a PhD in Psychometrics, which he received in 1969. Ironically, Nick may have avoided the draft because the Navy already had him on its rolls.

Nick thinks the reason he earned all these degrees was to prove himself, to make up for the feeling of being a failure when he was younger. And he was in fact ambitious and successful, leading an impressive career over several decades in educational testing and measurement. He taught research methods, multivariate analysis, and statistics in the Department of Education at Michigan State University, which is one of the strongest programs of its kind in the country. He then went to Berkeley to work with Glen Nimnicht, who directed the Far West Educational Research Laboratory, a Great Society program that sought to implement new ideas about how children learn. He was also teaching as an adjunct at the University of California at Berkeley, then became a visiting professor there as well. During this time he was developing evaluation and measurement techniques intended to supplement standardized testing protocols, and became nationally known as an evaluator who integrated humanistic techniques into educational testing. At Berkeley, he started by teaching courses in Inferential Statistics, but ended up designing a course in Humanistic Measurement Techniques. He also had a fellowship with the Stanford Research Institute, and spent time in Washington, DC, and elsewhere working to influence the way educational achievement is measured, pushing for a more humanistic approach, one that would take more of each student's background into account.

In 1981 the Educational Research Laboratory program ended and Nick wrote a federal grant to develop a curriculum for mainstreaming handicapped children into public education. Then over the next few years his life fell apart. Utterly exhausted by years of driven work, he went through a divorce and was diagnosed with multiple sclerosis. He returned the third year of funding for his new program to the government because the school system he was working with wasn't accepting the concept. Determined to heal himself and change his life, he turned to holistic medicine, started working only as a consultant to organizations, and in 1983 moved to Crested Butte full-time. He owned a house in the valley because his ex-in-laws had lived in Gunnison. They had told him to forget about Crested Butte because "There are strange people there." But one day in about 1972 he'd driven up the valley and discovered quickly, as he puts it, "These people were just like me!"

Over the next few years, Nick radically changed his life. He spent time at the monastery in Snowmass, chopping wood and carrying water, earning his living by traveling to consult, and deeply reevaluating who he was. By this point, he had a substantial national reputation in humanistic evaluation of complex organizational systems. At the same time he became more committed to his own art and to his health, and it began to improve. He co-authored a book with Crested Butte writer and editor Sandy Fails, *The Life-Planning*

Workbook, that drew on his experience in psychology with organizations, but focused that learning on individuals.

Nick lived in Crested Butte full-time for about twenty years, until he began to spend more time in Scottsdale to avoid the harsh winters. And slowly over the years, as he healed, even becoming stronger despite the progression of his MS, he unleashed his inner clown. He thinks the roots of his transformation lay in his uncle's barbershop back in New Jersey, where "they told jokes like crazy." In Crested Butte he got involved with the Mountain Theater and met Eric Ross, who used to act in Chicago's Second City (when he moved to Crested Butte, Eric's replacement was a young actor named John Belushi). Nick remembers going into local shops with Eric and firing off improvisational routines just to startle the tourists. In those days he says everyone participated in this kind of thing. So one July he and Pat Dawson—another gifted Crested Butte artist, a painter, and the mother of über-mountaineer Lou—decided that the Fourth of July parade needed clowns and they were the ones for the job. Over the years Nick kept clowning in the parade, adding on to his act, developing little routines and episodes, using a camera or flowers that shot water, handing out lollipops to children until he was giving away over a thousand and acquiring costumes and props. He started working with Six Points, the residential treatment and employment center for physically and mentally challenged adults in Gunnison, to involve them in the event.

Nick recalls that one of the scarier moments in his career as a clown was one summer when the Hell's Angels were in town. Nick went up to one during the parade and squirted him in the face with a trick flower. "There was a second there when I thought I might be in trouble," he says, "but then the guy just looked at me and laughed. See, it works. Clowning works."

Another one of Nick's recent projects is the restoration of the Old Adobe Mission in Scottsdale. The town grew up around the mission, which was built by Native Americans and Mexican immigrants in the 1930s. The building had been abandoned and was near collapse when Nick first saw it. Plans were to sell it or tear it down, but he thought about what it meant to local people and decided it needed to be saved. He spearheaded efforts to raise a small fortune, renovations began in 2004, and the old mission reopened several years later.

Looking back, Nick says, "The crisis in my life allowed me to get focused on what my true self was, and that was helping people in a way that was creative and caring and fulfilling." When he had been a driven academic and professional he feels that he wasn't doing that work in any way for himself, only to satisfy internal demons, and that is why he eventually crashed. Becoming a clown was part of the change, which was confirmed for him when he saw Marcel Marceau perform. Nick talked with Marceau after the show and he recalls Marceau told him he should keep clowning because one of the most fulfilling things in life is to make others feel happy. Now, Nick says, "It's my duty to make other people find their inner clown. Let there be clowns."

And there were clowns, clowns in the mountains. And it was good.

Interlude

Elegant Snowflake: A Haiku Sequence

The Art of Snow Viewing: An Intuitive View of Snow

Snow and avalanches, like all wonders of Nature, reveal themselves on micro and macro levels. Japanese artists, especially many of the ancient haiku poets, lived much of their lives in snow. By reading their poems one can begin to understand that the snow flake is much more than frozen water falling from the sky. We will explore these complex and elegant forms, the forces in our atmosphere and imagination which constantly drive this dynamic system. Along the way, we'll contemplate the poetry and metaphorical power of snow, and how mountain communities co-exist with and pay tribute to its destructive manifestation. No previous experience with snow, skiing or avalanche awareness is required.

—Advertisement for a poetry writing workshop

1.

The snow is falling.
I am really fucking drunk.
Why am I naked?

The snow is on me.
I am in a snow bank now.
It is very cold.

Beautiful snowflake,
Why are you stuck in my eye?
Fuck off, you snowflake.

In Colorado,
We think snow is beautiful.
We like vodka, too.

I need a blanket.
Where are the apartment keys?
I'd like a drink now.

Cherry blossom? What
Cherry blossom. I don't see
A cherry blossom.

Elegant snowflakes,
I can write my name in you
Like this: wee, wee, wee.

2.

Excuse me, mister.
Could you please help me to break
This stupid window?

Thanks, I'm ok, man.
It's my apartment. No keys.
That? It's my beacon.

I am wearing it
In case snow falls off that roof.
Look . . . batteries good.

No, most people don't
Wear avalanche beacons and
No shoes. Or clothing.

Did I tell you that
My girlfriend moved out today?
Hey, thanks for the ride.

Those flashing lights on
Your car are really cool, dude.
I don't have ID.

Still snowing. You know,
Snowflakes are more than
Frozen water. Shit.

3.

Why are you laughing?
Is it something that I said?
Her name is Ashley.

She left this bottle
Of vodka and so I drank
All of it. So there.

These clothes don't fit right.
Orange is not my color.
Sorry I threw up.

You guys are funny.
This bed is too hard for me.
But warmer than snow.

Do you like the snow?
I like skiing in the snow.
Let's all go skiing.

Ashley has great tits,
But sometimes she is so mean.
I'm getting sleepy.

Here is my beacon.
I think we can turn it off.
See you for breakfast.

Do me a favor?
Would one of you call Ashley,
And tell her that I

Drank all the vodka,
But that her cat is inside
And I forgive her

Because she is like
Snow, a wonder of nature,
That falls from the sky.

20

Kasha Rigby:
A Creative Way to Live

In the spring of 1993, Kasha Rigby was twenty-three years old, a waitress at the Grand Butte Hotel in Crested Butte. Having learned to ski at Stowe (where her parents own the Hob Knob, an inn on the road to the area), she watched the US Extreme Skiing Championships at the Butte the year before, and thought, "Well, I can do that." So when the Food and Beverage Department of Crested Butte Mountain Resort announced they were going to sponsor one entry, she decided to try out for it. Kasha says she did it "sort of as a joke," as she hadn't competed much in high school, but she won the sponsorship. She then went on to prove she could indeed do it, and took third overall in the women's division.

In and of itself, especially considering that she hadn't had very much competitive experience before such a big race, this is an impressive result. What gave it particular historical zing in the ski world, however, is the way Kasha earned it: on what we used to call "pins." She was the only competitor, male or female, even to make it to the final day of competition on telemark gear.

Kasha's podium not only amazed a lot of people—even the macho pinhead hardcores in Crested Butte, who began to pronounce her name in tones of hushed awe—but it ignited a predictable controversy. As Kasha tells it, "The first year, everyone was real nice to me, because they thought I wasn't any competition." Maybe they were fooled by the fact that she stands about 5'3" and looks and acts about as menacing as a sunny day. But after she smoked most of the field, there were complaints from other women competitors about how the judges couldn't evaluate telemark skiing fairly, that they had been cutting Kasha slack because she was using a free heel. As a result, in 1994, she didn't know if she would be allowed to compete until two days beforehand, and didn't have time to line up sponsorship money.

Fortunately for Kasha and our sport, some heavy lobbying by the likes of chief judge Jean Pavillard, a certified Swiss guide and at that time the director of the Crested Butte Ski School, convinced the rest of the judging committee to let Kasha in. The money problem remained, but the day she found out she would be allowed to compete, she went in to work at The Brick Oven, and they pulled out the checkbook on the spot.

This time there were three other telemarkers in addition to Kasha, all men. Kasha recalls that the judges, responding to last year's criticism, told them that they would judge the telemarkers particularly strictly. Hip checks and hand touches would be cause for any skier to be marked down. One of the men made it to the second day, but then switched to alpine gear on day two, lost a ski, and was eliminated.

Kasha took fourth (not fifth, as some other sources have written—"Let's get that straight," she says). If anything, the controversy seems to have fired her up. "I wanted to ski well, to be technically clean, not only for myself, but for the sport, to show that telemarking has a place in this event. I felt that if I blew it this year, everyone would say 'we told you so, she's getting judged unfairly.' But I skied really well, hitting all the lines I wanted."

Stowe, Kasha's hometown, still isn't associated with telemarking and the sport was minuscule there in the mid-1980s when Kasha first tried it. She started because one day when she was in tenth grade, a boyfriend showed up to ski on telemark gear. "I was so embarrassed. I thought he was a geek. But I wanted him to think I was cool, so I tried it too, on rental gear. I loved it from the beginning, though it took me quite a while before I totally switched over—not until I moved to Colorado. But in my high school, where almost all the skiers were racers, people thought I had become a freak of nature."

By 1994, the other competitors at the Extremes probably didn't think of Kasha's skiing as freaky. But her world-class results in an event often dominated by serious attitude belied her self-effacing, friendly, and unpretentious manner. When I asked her why she didn't go to the Worlds after her great showing in '93, she said, "Well, it didn't occur to me that anyone would pay for me to go."

As Heather Talbot, one of her ski buddies in those days put it, "I've never seen her ski without a smile on her face. She does it for herself because she gets so much out of it." And Jessica James, who grew up with Kasha in Stowe and now patrols at Snowmass, says Kasha "never admits to how good she is. The week after the Extremes I was in CB. We'd be walking down the street, and locals were all over her, inviting her into bars for free drinks, and so on, and she would brush it off. Someone was in town to make a ski film, invited her to be in it, and she blew it off just to ski with me. She'd rather ski with her friends than stand around waiting for the sun to come out." I'd have to agree with that. After she started winning, talking to her in public became difficult, as some guy would always be coming up and interrupting to say something like, "Hey Kasha, if I crawl on my hands and knees through broken glass will you go skiing with me?"

Kasha is one of those people who talks more about love for the sport than the competitive scene. When I asked her about her plans in those days, her first response was to say she wants to do a lot more backcountry skiing. Then, after a pause in that interview so long ago, she said she also wanted to improve her technical climbing, the better to get to the places she wants to ski. She summed it up by saying, "I just want to ski everywhere!" all of which she then did and continues to do.

Back in the 1990s, Kasha said that the fact that she was getting sick of serving hamburgers to pay rent might push her to try to capture more of the limelight she had earned in competition, and she told me that she'd like to do the Extremes again, put more energy into the telemark gate racing scene, and go to the Worlds ("But that's still a money thing," she added).

* * *

I don't know where Kasha is now. We haven't been in touch in many years. I heard a few years back that she got married, quit skiing and moved away somewhere to raise a family. That led me to do a quick internet search in spring 2012 that brought up a photo of her, Hilaree Nelson, Margaret Wheeler, and another Crested Butte skier, Alison Gannett, all wearing sunglasses, black sports bras, and smiles, on the summit of India's 5,984-meter Hanuman Tibba before their successful first descent just a few years ago. She's a sponsored athlete with the North Face, and still as beautiful and charming as ever—and now sporting an alpinist resume that includes dozens of major ascents and first descents all over the planet. I think she is married, with kids, living in Salt Lake . . . but obviously still living the ski and alpinist life. I should look her up.

Now in her forties, Kasha has had a substantial impact on the sport for twenty years, bringing telemark technique into a competitive arena where no one thought it could be done. It's fair to say she changed the sport. But in talking to her all those years ago, I was even more impressed by her passion for skiing pure and simple, unencumbered by judges, clocks, and fame, and that pure attitude seems to hold true today. In an interview posted online that was shot as part of *The Edge of Never*, a film based on Bill Kerig's book of the same name about Kye Petersen, Kasha closes by talking about her time in the mountains with her companions and says:

> It's this constant search for balance in life. But so often I'm in the mountains with people that I just love so much that I'm just right there with them . . . and that's our great love affair right there . . . being there in the mountains together, and getting in and getting out together.

As long as our sport continues to attract people like this, at least part of it will stay what it was always meant to be: a creative way to live.

21

Sartorial Styles of the Butte

Recently, I visited a nearby resort town which will remain nameless. Let us call it "Deadwood." As I was strolling the immaculate streets and malls of Deadwood, wandering through art galleries that have paintings so expensive one wonders why they aren't in the Louvre and shops that sport jewelry so big it belongs on a weight rack at the gym, I happened to pick up the current issue of a magazine I will call *Deadwood Tripper*. It was hard to pick up, like that jewelry, because it was 254 pages of 9x11 glossy stock, but pick it up I did. I needed the exercise.

Inside the front cover, on the first page of the magazine, was a full-page ad for a company that shall remain nameless. Let us call it "The South Cheek." It was an ad tailored to the aspirations of Deadwood. It showed a buffed young woman running down a muddy trail, sunglasses propped on her forehead to insure retina damage, wearing a long-sleeved red zip-up, khaki pants, a pack, and running shoes. The clothes were immaculate. I could see the crease on the new pants. The shoes looked like they had just been cleaned by a federal agricultural customs inspection officer. The ad copy read as follows:

> Other tourists will be asking you for directions because you
> look so good wearing The South Cheek. The next best thing
> to being a local is gearing up like one. The latest tech, the
> latest look, the best prices. We've got it all. And we won't
> tell anyone where you just flew in from. Stop by one of our
> convenient slopeside locations and we'll help you fit in.

I stopped in my tracks and began ranting in public. "What?" I said
to my wife. "What? Look at this!"

My family started sidling away, not, it should be pointed out, for
the first time. They knew what was coming. "Oh, him? Never saw
him before in my life . . . Says he's a performance artist—"

Fair enough. There I stood, giggling and weeping like a hungry,
stoned, couch-surfing, dredlocked telemarker who's just broken a
binding on the first run of a powder day. "Is this what it's come to?"
I asked no one in particular, my eyes bulging, my arms gesticulating
wildly. My family had snuck out the door, cringing. But I gamely continued, now to no one in particular: "I mean, come on! Campy, coy,
self-mocking advertisements shilling overpriced, high-status, faux
rugged-fashion Gore-Tex to poseurs who drive their Ford Lexapro
to the mall? What is going *on* here, people?" No one answered my
questions. But that's fine—they were rhetorical questions.

The nice thing about rhetorical questions is that you get to
answer them yourself. And my answer is that things may well in
fact have arrived at such an unbalanced state in Deadwood, but
not in Crested Butte. Life may be changing, but Buttians still like
unconventional tailoring, sartorial funk, eccentric haberdashery,
utilitarian togs, even when dressed up, and the gifted local pho-
tographers can prove it.

What you see on the following pages are pictures of people

who did not just fly in. They are not trying to fit in to anything, as far as I can tell. It's not hard to figure out how to buy what they're wearing. Here's a tip: it's useful or creative or comfortable or fun, and the people wearing it like it that way.

So lose the stretchy bike shirt with the logos of all those companies who never heard of you—what are you, a billboard?—put on your Margaret Mead horn rims and study the following photos and stories carefully, as they represent the native dress of Butteworld, an island of fashion sanity in an ocean of mendacity, an authentic sartorial culture unsullied by haute couture, where the natives still know how to get dressed by themselves.

This is Al Smith, working the barbecue at the top of Painter Boy / Gold Link on the last day of the ski season in 2006. Al is the owner of Camp 4 Coffee, which now has cafés all over the upper valley, including one at the top of the Gold Link lift when this photo was

PHOTO BY TOM STILLO

taken. Al's coffee is good. He is responsible for more nervous chatter than anyone else in Crested Butte. And he's an energetic guy himself. Politicians tremble when they sense his approach. And he wears shorts all winter. Want to fit in? Try that.

Al is wearing a straw hat and some stubble, along with a very nice shirt, an old blue vest and a dirty apron. The apron is dirty because Al is working. Many recent studies show that working is a good way to fit in to a community.

As you can see, this was a beautiful day. Unlike the South Cheek model in *Deadwood Tripper*, Al is actually wearing his sunglasses. That's because the sun is out.

What an afternoon we had up there. All the young bucks were at other parties scattered around the hill, drinking more than is reasonable and doing their best to jump off stuff and wind up drooling on a gurney. The top of Gold Link featured peace and quiet, families, small kids, sunshine, moderate consumption of cold beer and outstanding bratwursts and burritos. And the skiing was splendid. We all fit in just fine. Thanks for a great lunch, Al.

PHOTO BY TOM STILLO

This is Tuck. He's a big, incredibly ripped dude wearing nothing except ski boots and tattoos. As you can see, he's in a "tuck." That's an inside joke—if you lived in our town, you'd be laughing by now.

After a career in the military and then in the police back east, Tuck moved here many years ago. He still teaches karate and drives the bus, skills which go well together on those rare occasions when passengers do silly things and deserve to have the stuffing kicked out of them. He also entertains at bachelorette parties in exactly this outfit (albeit sans boots). And I think he likes me, so y'all better treat me right. I know he likes my wife, because he once told her in Clark's grocery store, when she was wearing Hot Chili Pepper pants after a run, that he wanted to smear honey all over her legs and lick it off. Hey, it's a small town, we're all friends.

Tuck is also a fine actor, a staple of the Mountain Theatre, especially the Shakespeare productions, where he often plays major roles.

As for the suit he's wearing, you don't need to buy it—you already own one yourself. The question is whether or not you have the moxie to, er, pull it off.

This is Heli Mae Peterson heading north on 2nd St., between Whit-

erock and Sopris around Christmastime. She is riding on solid ice, holding on with one hand while she walks the dog with the other and gazes away from her line of travel to smile at the photographer. Think this is easy? I think it makes Nadia Comaneci look like a spaz. On top of all that, Heli is looking stylish in blue jeans and a lovely sweater. I doubt the flowers on the basket are real, but it's a nice touch when it's so cold that door handles are breaking off.

PHOTO BY TOM STILLO

Helie Mae is co-owner, with her sister Kay, of Donita's, where you can get a great Tex-Mex dinner, a delicious margarita, and see who's dating who. If you want to catch up on the latest tech, maybe you can even convince Heli to give you lessons in single-handed ice biking.

If you think this is a posed shot, go back to Deadwood (notice the dog is panting).

PHOTO BY MARK REAMAN

Presenting Jackson Melnick, twelve when this photo was snapped, who was in my older son's class at the public school. Jackson is making a ski turn in his sneakers on a steep summer snowfield littered with rocks and avalanche debris while holding a large pine branch à la Al Johnson, old-school. He is also looking stylish in a green T-shirt and shorts. No helmet, though. Jackson, where was your dad?

Telemark skiing has become big business, and many people who practice it today don't know that Crested Butte is one of the places where the free-heel turn was reborn about forty years ago. But I bet Jackson knows. Though here he does seem to be making a Cristiana turn. What's up with that, Jackson?

If you don't live in a mountain town and you have children, show them this picture and see if what they talk about is the fact that Jackson doesn't look cool because he isn't wearing designer togs. I'm fairly confident of the outcome of this question. Then ask them if they'd rather hang out with Jackson or spend the summer at the mall.

One more thing: just to confuse preconceptions a bit, you should know that when former Supreme Court Justice Sandra Day O'Connor visited Crested Butte the next summer, Jackson came to her public talk and asked a tough question about her vote in the Gore case. He appeared quite calm at the microphone. That's what learning to make a ski turn in sneakers before your voice even drops can do for you. Teaches you how to stay cool under fire.

This is the former Mayor of Crested Butte, Alan Bernholtz, chairing a Town Council meeting. The town staff constructed this ramp

PHOTO BY CHRIS LADOULIS

as a demonstration for the public of an Elk Avenue business that would comply with the new Horizontal Zoning regulations. After landing safely and extinguishing himself, Bernholtz commented, "We all want a vibrant downtown. And what could be more vibrant than a politician dressed in a Soul Train costume jumping off a burning ramp of snow attached to a truck on the main drag of town? That ought to sell a few T-shirts."

To be fair, Alan did this before becoming Mayor, but he was on the Town Council at the time. Contemplating the cultural significance of this picture, I'd like to suggest that if every municipality in the country required something comparable from all office-holders, we'd probably be building a stronger, safer America. At least we'd confuse our enemies. "I apologize, Mr. President, I cannot explain it. Perhaps it is part of their religion. I think he is trying to become a martyr."

Actually, this photo comes from our Mardi Gras celebration (I guess that does make it religious after all). Alan is hucking himself in blue sequins and those beads that always wind up on trees near chairlifts. That is not his own hair. As you can see, his constituents are pleased with his performance.

Alan fits in. Now, what he is doing may look easy, but the consequences of failure are high and might involve reconstructive surgery on your face. After a few shots at the Eldo, you too may think you can fly burning through the air at dusk and run this town, but you should know that Alan was not only Mayor but is also an experienced alpinist and the owner of Crested Butte Mountain Guides. Ah, Grasshopper, there is a difference between merely sporting the latest tech and stomping a skinny landing on concrete at dusk while blinded by a smoking fright wig.

Here we have Nan Lumb and Pat Dawson in full-on Crested Butte formal wear at the 2006 annual Black and White Ball, which is a fundraiser for the Heritage Museum. That's Harvey Castro in the

background wearing the groovy top hat. The building that houses the museum is on Elk Avenue, and was formerly the home, for many decades, of Tony's Conoco, a hardware store and gas station that Tony Mihelich ran every day until his death a decade ago when he was in his late nineties. Thanks to the hard work of many people in the community, the building has been lovingly restored and has become a town institution.

PHOTO BY MARK REAMAN

Nan and Pat have both lived in Crested Butte for a long time. Nan runs 418 Elk, a stylish shop a block away from the museum; Pat is an artist whose work is viewable all over town. Her son, Lou, lived in town in the 1970s, and then went on to be the first person to ski from the summit of all fifty-four peaks above fourteen thousand feet in the state. In 2005 he was inducted into the Colorado Ski Hall of Fame.

As for the clothes—well, when we talk about black tie philanthropic functions here, it's a bit different from the New York Yacht Club. There's a bit more latitude to the definitions, an active encouragement of a certain *je ne sais quoi*. As you can tell, Nan and Pat are having fun, in the spirit of CB's many dress-up functions. Note the empty wine glasses.

Most places just have Halloween. Crested Butte has the Al Johnson Race, Flauschink, Vinotok, the Red Lady Ball, Winter Carnival, Mardi Gras, and more. Pearls are great (as long as you don't hook them on a T-Bar), but so is a psychedelic hat.

Looking good, ladies. Pat, I like the pink streak. Are you going punk?

PHOTO BY TOM STILLO

In this photo Ben Somrak is not dressed up as a firefighter. He *is* a firefighter. He doesn't wear these clothes to look cool, but rather to stay cool when he is hauling your unconscious body out of a burning building. As for fitting in like Ben, give it up. He's a fifth-generation Buttician. His family has been in the valley for over a century. He also is the co-founder of Two Plank Productions, a sports film-making company, and he skis like a bandit. This is not the kind of thing you can *buy*. You have to *live* it. This young man is not only the past of Crested Butte, but also its present and its future.

Ben is smiling because it is the Fourth of July and he is riding high in the annual parade. He knows that in a few minutes he's going to be in the middle of an enormous water fight between First and Second Avenue, and he's got the advantage of height, an escape vehicle, and heavy artillery. You'd smile too. And he also knows that the Town Council is going to clean up after the parade. After the parade and the water fight, they come in with gloves and shovels, picking up what the horses have left behind and throwing it in the scoop of a front loader.

Our town council takes a lot of heat. You should have seen the fight one year over horizontal zoning, evidence that in Crested Butte democracy remains an ongoing contact sport, perhaps a combination of rugby and darts. But that's not a bad thing. The town remains an experiment in how people can live peacefully together and pursue happiness. Sort of like Brook Farm with an attitude. And folks generally work things out because they all take part in one way or another. So now, having vented my spleen, I should end in that spirit of cooperation and community with a more civil invitation. If you really want to fit in to such a place, even if you're just visiting, don't worry about your clothes, don't fret about the latest tech.

The best way to fit in is to join in. Come as you are. Here's your shovel.

22

Ripping with Jake

Kids who grow up in ski towns have a warped view of the world, believing that most of it is tilted and covered with snow eight months a year. My son Jacob and his friends were on Crested Butte's North Face at the age of six. We parents would ski behind them, watching them slither and slide over the bumps on Hawk's Nest like ladybugs. You had to be careful—if they fell, they would disappear from sight.

Jacob's favorite sports are mountain biking and running. He doesn't ski race any more, and has become a competitive distance runner in college. But skiing comes as naturally to him as walking, which isn't too surprising since he started both at about the same time. I've watched him grow into it, trying to support him but to keep a distance, to let him discover it for himself. And now that he's nineteen, I'm grateful for our many days together: the first time hiking the peak of Crested Butte above the lifts, when he was the youngest person up there by a decade; the first time we skied Rambo together, hopping over the exposed logs on the top of the fifty-degree entrance; a day at Snowbird when he was only ten and it had snowed forty inches overnight, road closed, tram open—and he skied it, looking a bit like a small ermine bounding through drifts as we drifted down Mach Schnell and Restaurant Row. Snaking through the tight trees on the back of Crested Butte's Horseshoe in the late spring, a few inches of the fresh still untracked mid-morning.

The April Jacob was twelve we were at a race in Breckenridge, a late-season Kombi, meaning that part of the race is slalom, part GS—a fun event for young racers, a way to change it up. After a long warm spell, the weather had turned, the temperature had dropped thirty degrees and it had snowed a foot, with high winds. On the lower part of Peak 10, the course was a rutted slab of tungsten. But I had a premonition that the famous Breckenridge hurricane might have created better conditions up high, a suspicion confirmed by the sound of bombing all morning.

The race ended early, I grabbed Jake and we headed for the T-Bar and Imperial Bowl. Riding Imperial it was obvious up above that the wind had been pouring dense deposition onto the lee aspects all night. Creamy windbuff as far as the eye could see, hardly a soul in sight, the clouds breaking up. Just my son and me, swinging on a chairlift at 12,500'. We got off at the top; I told him to follow and picked the most direct line. The tips of a few, gray, frozen moguls were still visible but easily avoidable and the snow would support anything in any direction, at high speed. It was a thousand verts of carveable velvet, bad turns were not for sale, and it was impossible to resist opening the throttle and heading for the bottom.

He can't get lost, I told myself. One lift, one run. He'll figure it out.

Ninety seconds later, thighs burning, I pulled up a hundred feet or so above the maze, on the flats, looking back up the hill for Jacob. I could see the entire bowl, but there was no sign of him anywhere. I knew he'd jumped in behind me, I knew there was no exit anywhere on the way down, and so I quickly began to think about explanations for his mother. Alien abduction? Spontaneous combustion?

A fraction of a second later I heard the whoosh and dull roar of a body and skis at speed and looked over my shoulder back down the hill to see Jake pulling out of a big, roundhouse turn that sent him back up the hill to me. He'd been that close. He skied up, timing his arc to stop at my side, grinning like he'd just gotten away with a lifestyle felony, or perhaps as though he'd just ripped a thousand verts of wind-buff at forty miles per hour.

"That was cool," he said. "Can we do it again?"

Before that moment, everything about being a father had meant protecting, leading, teaching. Without warning, all of that began to shift, to pivot, to change. Spontaneous combustion indeed. Who was this young guy?

I thought, what a pleasure it's going to be to find out. While I can still keep up.

"Yeah," I said, heading for the lift, "Yeah, let's do it again."

JACOB ROTHMAN, AGE 14, BACK OF MT. OWEN, 2008.
PHOTO BY DAVID J. ROTHMAN.

Part Three

Living the Life

23

Breaking Trail

The first time I broke trail—really broke trail—was about fifteen years ago, when Steph and Harry were visiting from Boulder and we went up to the Elkton Hut. It snowed buckets on top of a stable spring snowpack. The snow was so good that on the way back down the valley the next day, Steph and I decided to do a bonus lap on Coney's, a steep, wooded ridge that tops out at about eleven thousand feet. I found the ghost of an old track and started climbing.

I've never been a fast climber and probably never will be. At least, I'm not fast by Crested Butte standards. Fast in Crested Butte means guys like Jimmy Faust, Dave Penney, Bryan Wickenhauser, Geo Bullock and Xavi Fanier. In February 2006, Jimmy and Canadian Greg Hill tied for first place in the 24 Hours of Sunlight race, climbing, transitioning, and skiing at the relaxed pace of 2,085 vertical feet per hour *for twenty-four hours straight* and topping the fifty thousand-foot mark by the time they stopped the clock. In the same race, Dave was fourth and Bryan was seventh. Still think you're fast?

And they're just the famous guys. What this boils down to is that I don't usually break trail. Or didn't used to.

But on this day, when Steph and I started climbing, it became clear that the old skin track was too steep. This is one of my pet peeves—the bad etiquette of putting in a track as steep as a cog railway. Fun on the first lap, useless by the third. There was less snow down at Coney's than up at the head of the valley, and we were slipping, the track more like a Hot Wheels chute than a good climb. We were working our way through the pines and neither of us was having much fun, so I just branched off and began slogging along.

The terrain at Coney's is complex. As you approach, it's clear enough—a wide, uniform ridge, heavily forested until it opens to the ski terrain further up the valley. But once you're on the wooded climbing pitch, you can't see where you're going, so you have to have some sense of the topography to hit the crest near your chosen line. I'd skied it many times and knew a number of markers, so I was comfortable with that.

The strange thing was that as I climbed and led, I seemed only to get stronger. So many other times at the front of the pack I'd felt uncomfortable—not experienced enough, not fast enough, not familiar enough with the terrain. But now, with each step, I had a sense of where we were, of where we were going, of what line to choose and of how to pace the climb. Before me, unbroken snow stretched upwards through the pines. It was my responsibility to pick the good spot for a turn, to avoid the terrain traps, to take the best route for our destination.

Something in me woke up, a faculty I'd hardly known I'd been developing. I felt more alive than ever as I headed uphill. I was the one making the decisions and someone else was depending on me. But more than that—I was depending on myself, as well. It was different and more complex than a corn tour, more three-dimensional. It was a bit like writing, choosing again and again what to lay down on a fresh page.

We crested and had an outstanding run with scores of turns

in the fresh. Steph is an old friend and a strong skier, and we had that kind of fun, relaxed tour that comes with knowing the terrain, trusting your partner, feeling safe and finding great snow. It was far from being the biggest or best ski either of us had ever had. But it was memorable because on that climb I could feel something coming to fruition, something I'd never really thought about but had somehow learned without realizing it.

This is how it happens. You wake up one day and even though you can name the stages and steps you went through to get where you are, you surprise yourself, you're changed, you've discovered something you hardly knew existed before that day, even though it was plainly in view.

I'm still slow, by hard core standards. I'll never be a professional guide. But now I love to break trail, not because I love being in the lead, though I do enjoy showing friends around. It's more about the relationship that breaking trail gives with a mountain, with a day, with the group.

Even now, in the heat of a June afternoon, I can imagine it, and it has a particular flavor. We are standing in a gently angled field, looking up onto the steep flank of the range where there is a forest, and above that the summit, where spindrift billows. We have just taken a break, shouldering our packs to set out. It's my turn to lead. People laugh and say, "Good! This won't be too fast . . ."

I look up, think for a few seconds. And then choose.

24

Going Solo

"Hi," said a tall, skinny guy. New to the group, he seemed nervous, kept playing with his plastic water glass. He laughed self-consciously. "Never done this before . . . Well . . . My name is John and . . . I go solo."

"Hi, John."

He sighed. "It didn't used to be this way. I started out with small things. You know, climbing a hill near the house alone. Soon I wanted more—ridge tops, smaller peaks below treeline, then distant glades. I was sneaking away for a couple of hours at a time, pretending I was only going to go part way. Just a few turns. Then, one day I skied a fourteener alone." He smiled. "It was *killer*. The beauty, the freedom, the—" His voice trailed off and he looked around like a dog that knows it's been bad.

"I admit it," he went on, "I'm an addict. Moonlight tours far from town, solo peaks at dawn. Even deep snow on steep aspects when the stability looks good." Heads around the room were nodding. "I know it's wrong. But I can't wait for my next fix . . . the thin, cold air. The secret rush of danger and guilt . . . I feel so . . . powerless."

Uh, what? Excuse me, time for a reality check.

Imagine climbing through the aspens, then up into the pines. A breeze rustles the branches, spilling snow from a few days ago. There's nothing to say as the crystals hang in the air, sparkling like diamonds. The sun flickers through the branches and the snow. You are alone with the world, with yourself, with the future, the past, and most importantly, the present.

That's no generic memory. I'm thinking of a time last year when I discovered a steep but beautifully safe glade on the north face of Snodgrass, a small mountain just outside of Crested Butte. Over the years I'd glimpsed what looked like a few openings in a stand of large older trees, and with the tender snowpack that day I wanted a line with absolutely no starting zone. Leaving the usual route, I started thrashing around in the woods, exploring on long traverses and then . . . deep in the heart of that forest appeared a series of linked glades in big, mature pines that had suppressed any under-growth. The line, which I named "Windows," was invisible from below or above, dropped five hundred vertical feet at about thir-ty-five degrees and was safer than a bank vault. It was bliss—snow to the knees, steep pitch, big trees, total silence except for the glisse of one powder skier.

When we are with others we inevitably focus a good part of our energy on them, and that is one way to be in the wilderness. A good way. But when other people are absent the mind becomes different, opening outward from isolation to take in more. Each tiny event—the flight of a ptarmigan across your line; the tracks of a snowshoe hare; a cyclone of snow swirling up the hillside; the gurgle of water from a buried stream—resonates even further, like a Zen bell. Alone, I become deeply aware of these things that con-tinue without me.

There's something primal and powerful about being on your own in the backcountry. Call it the Outward Bound Impulse, or the

Messner Mindset. It's almost a spiritual discipline, one where you are absolutely responsible for yourself in every way: your choices, your experience, your safety, your adrenaline, your food, your feelings, your thoughts. It can be anti-social and dangerous, but the same could be said for having a glass of wine or reading a book. It's all a matter of how and why it's done.

There are some who probably don't want you to think about this too much. These folks would be the ones who want to control and limit as many aspects of your life as you're willing to surrender without a fight. I can hear them whispering, like an anxious little conscience: "No, no! Don't do it! It's irresponsible! Remember our image with the public. They think we're crazy as it is!" And that's fair enough. In America many of us already look like renegades. Bearded guys with dilated pupils, girls who don't shave, etc. We remind people of that nutty guy in John Krakauer's *Into the Wild*.

But most of us are not like that. Solo winter wilderness alpine excursions are something many of us just do. For backcountry skiers who have been practicing for a decade or more, going solo evolves naturally out of lengthy experience, difficult to convey to a larger public not familiar with alpinism. That's how it happened for me. I grew into it over time as I learned the hundreds of little technical skills that eventually add up to expertise: what clothes to bring, what route to climb, what line to ski, what is going on in the snowpack, how to make an uphill kick-turn, where the weather is headed, and so much more.

Watershed moments are spiritual, not technical. One came for me when mountain guide Jean Pavillard said over dinner—with rapture in his eyes—that the night before, under a full moon, he had skied three laps solo on Coney's, an eleven thousand foot ridge several miles up Washington Gulch. It seemed, if not a reasonable thing to do, at the very least a good thing to do, a beautiful thing to do. And I yearned to do it too. Solo.

Like reading or practicing a musical instrument, ski mountaineering has a deeply inward and individual component. It's profoundly American in a rebellious sort of way even though many Americans still have trouble understanding it, thanks to our emphasis on team and spectator sports, or worse, an over-emphasis on safety. Even mountain biking and rock climbing usually take place on routes made by others. Wilderness skiing, on the other hand, offers isolation of a different order. It demands choice with every movement. Alone, you can go anywhere those choices lead you. If that means that certain entities wish to see us as "irresponsible," well, we may just have to live with that.

Here's a test—if going solo seems to you like an adventure that will add excitement to what you're doing, it may not be a good idea. If, on the other hand, it becomes just another choice, one that grows out of a desire for solitude and silence, one way to be in the mountains among others, something to do when the time is right—then maybe you're ready.

So let there be no more apologies for going solo. Perhaps I'll see your solo tracks or you'll see mine, and in that way, without even knowing each other, we will come to a deeper appreciation of each other's solitude. To know that you have already been here or will come after, in search of the same kind of wild, inspiring seclusion, might provide us with a kind of communion. For me, after such an adventure, I ski home to the valley with its human joys, sorrows, and obligations, deeply revitalized.

Talk to me. How about you?

25

The Kids Are Alright

Visitors to Crested Butte invariably come round to asking what it's like to raise children in a mountain town. The way the question comes out can be revealing. You can tell that your interlocutors are wistfully imagining ditching their upscale yuppie jobs and escaping to paradise. She's beginning to think that a pile sweater covered with dog hair really can look ok in some colors, and he's thinking, well, running a restaurant can't be *that* much work . . . but there's a problem. Charlie is eleven and Becca is eight. They're in a good school. He plays the violin and needs braces and she's on the swim team and they both have lots of friends. The parents are willing to make a lifestyle choice but if the environment here isn't good for the children, then the deal's off. And when it comes to moving to a small mountain town, you can understand by the look in the parents' eyes that, while they've had a good time on the North Face or Trail 401, they're not sure the valley is actually civilized. So when they ask, "So . . . uh, what are the schools like?" the body language sometimes suggests that the real question is if kids in this town ever say "please" and know that you're supposed to wash fruit before you eat it.

It's tempting to take the easy way out here and say, "Of course our kids say 'please,' especially when asking for another toke," but I want to keep you guessing. I might make lists of relevant data points like test scores in the local schools, where to get flu shots, how many piano teachers there are, and I could print pictures of brightly scrubbed children laughing as they rinse apples in filtered water. Near background: national historic district. Far dissolve: alpine playground.

Sorry. Instead, I'm going to tell some stories.

Let's begin with language, that profound communal artifact. Every parent knows that a threshold in family life is crossed when a child learns the power of a single syllable: "No!" I remember vividly how this development occurred with my second son, Noah. On the magical day when he learned how to assert himself in the negative, he didn't say "No."

He said, "No way."

At least he didn't call me "dude."

I found this pretty funny, and now when he says it I have to confess I sometimes can't resist replying "Way," because he then says, "No way! No way!" I then calmly respond, "Way," which annoys him, even though he does know it is in fact time for him to get in the car to go to preschool, which makes him start screaming, "No way no way no way no way!" as he stands on his toes and turns red in the face, even though he loves his preschool, which makes me start laughing. At this point my wife asks me what, exactly, I think I'm accomplishing, which is a reasonable question.

That commute down to the Little Red Schoolhouse, a wonderful preschool in CB South, was generally the farthest we ever had to take our children (orthodonture appointments and athletic competitions excepted). This differs from the last place we lived, where, in a brief attempt to escape the vortex of beautiful mountain life and reconnect with post-industrial neo-urban America—an extended visit to the set of *The Stepford Wives*—my wife Emily drove so much she considered buying a chauffeur's cap. She estimates she was behind the wheel upwards of fifty miles every day just to shuttle our two boys around. When you do this, your children may learn the model numbers of every vehicle in the current production line of the big four, but that's time they might otherwise be spending playing in Coal Creek or throwing snowballs or learning to fend for themselves a little bit, become residents of their own commu-nity by traveling it on foot and bike rather than zipping around in machines. Young children don't segment time and experience the way adults do and they learn from everything, including how they move through the world. Your choice. Go ahead, keep driving.

I can feel your fear. "You . . . *let your children ride their bikes around town? By themselves?*" Yes, we do. By the time they're ten or eleven years old, most children in Crested Butte know the rules and follow them because they live in a culture where riding bikes is the norm, not the exception. Further, they know how to ride bikes. Many of them have grown up on skis and bikes and by that age are riding single-track trails like Snodgrass, Strand Hill, the Upper Loop, and even 401 (yes, those are the easier ones).

It's the same with skiing. By the time they're six, Crested Butte kids ski things that no one thought were even skiable a generation ago. The biggest problem I can recall in skiing with my older son Jacob when he was younger was that he was so light that when he and his friend Jackson would try to ride the old poma up to the North Face, it would pick them up and dangle them like hooked trout, much to the amusement of the hard cores assembled in line.

"Yo, check out that little dude, he's getting like, huge air . . . "

"Whoah, that is so sick. . . ."

Richard, Jackson's dad, and I eventually hit on the scheme of having our six-year-old sons wear our backpacks as they rode the lift, which solved the levitation problem but made them look like diminutive sherpas, raising the specter of being reported to Social Services. All this so that children who don't yet know their multiplication tables can ski Body Bag Glades.

When he got a bit older, Jacob would ask me if we could "do a rocket" when we rode the North Face T-Bar together, which meant angling our skis a bit to hold the T back until the cable played all the way out and then, when we let go, launched us forward like . . . well, like a rocket. I would tell him no, we can't do that, first because I don't weigh eighty-five pounds and we might derail the T-bar, and second, because it might make disk fluid squirt out of my back, and he should save the thrills for skiing Phaser and Cesspool, but by then of course the cable had played out, he had sneakily set his edges, and we'd be airborne. Why didn't I remember how that works? Ouch.

The climate does present challenges. Dressing toddlers when it's twenty below takes about ninety minutes and resembles solving a Rubik's Cube. It requires the correct layering of diaper, long underwear, fleece pants, wool shirt, sweater, snow pants, jacket, hat, goggles, and mittens, a labor of love which inevitably leads to that charming moment when the little bundle of joy, who now resembles the Michelin Man, waddles up to you and says, "Daddy? I have to go pee—"

Given their ease in the physical world, most local children know their way around. Wherever they are, friends are always nearby. Crested Butte is a village and children do not move anonymously through their own lives. If children do something foolish, someone they know will generally see it and perhaps correct it. Of course, that person will probably not only tell you, but also inform a number of your friends, which can be annoying. But heck, I could tell you some pretty good stories myself. Everyone has a part to play in keeping shame-based culture alive.

Village life is a notion that everyone claims to understand, but people who have not experienced it cannot fully grasp what it's like. The devil is in the details. There are obviously a number of amenities Crested Butte does not have—an art museum stuffed with Monets, a high school orchestra, a drugstore, a Ferris wheel, a local chapter of the Crips—but what it does have is precious. When Jacob would leave to play with his friends Sarah and Kai Sherman, I knew that their father, Roger, was also Jacob's doctor (and an experienced partner in the backcountry who sings beautiful old Tin Pan Alley standards with me when I play piano on Friday nights at the Elk Mountain Lodge) and his wife, Susan, was a gifted nurse who had been present when Jacob was born (even though she wasn't on-duty), and was present for Noah seven years later, and while Emily was recovering Sue gave Noah his first bath. And just as I help Roger out with chromaticism when he's learning jazz tunes, he'll come down and look in a child's ear or listen to his chest if we ask him to.

And when Noah would get together with his friend Richie to laugh and break toys, I knew that his mother Holly is a great cook who used to own Cookworks and his father, Dan, was at that time the Head of the Slate River School, which enjoyed a run as an excellent K-6 private independent day school in town, and I know what a wonderful educator and person he is because he was a history teacher, the dean of Student Life, director of Outdoor Education and about twenty-seven other things at Crested Butte Academy when I was Head there, and did a great job. Oh, and he's a great backcountry partner too. And plays a mean guitar.

And when Jacob would be working on middle-school English, I knew that one of the teachers in the school was Pat O'Neill, who not only has won the Grand Traverse (which qualifies him an über-backcountry partner), but who also once invited me to guest-teach one of his high school classes and is a cracker-jack educator, among many others at the public school, which in those days included Maggie McCarty, Jake's music teacher, a singer, someone else with whom I'd played some music. She sang Irving Berlin's "Cheek to Cheek" and did a good job. Then there's Danny Albin, who drives heavy machinery in town and is as strong as a horse. The first time I met him was teaching a class on Chaucer as a guest lecturer for a day in the high school. Danny is big and Danny didn't like Chaucer, something he let me know repeatedly. But I later learned that Danny knows just about every single fact there is to know about the American Civil War—more than I ever will—and now, many years after that fateful day when I practically threw him out of class, he's as sweet to me as a summer's day. He's a lovely guy and still someone I'd want on my side in a fight.

And when Jacob and Noah would go to class at the Crested Butte School of Dance, I knew that the co-Director, Bobbie Reinhardt, was a wonderful teacher because she was also a neighbor and has taught primary school music in the public school for decades, and her son, Eric, is a gifted graduate of Crested Butte Academy who went on to be the captain of the Dartmouth Ski Team. If you want to see a true community lovefest, come see the School of Dance's annual show in May, which usually sells out the Center for the Arts for several performances and is probably the biggest event of the off-season.

All of this reminds me of a night Jacob spent at a friend's opulent home during our *Stepford Wives* period. Of course we didn't know the family. And I have nothing against them. But when Jake came home the next morning and his mother asked him how it had been, he said "It was so cool. We never really saw the parents. They just got us McDonald's for dinner and we got to eat it in these reclining chairs in front of the Gameboy in like this private theater room, and we watched a lot of movies and slept there too, on those chairs. It was really fun. Dad . . . is something the matter?"

Children in a real mountain town have a very different kind of life than they would in or near any city. Because a place like Crested Butte is a village, they become citizens of it at an earlier age. They have their own reputations and relations with all sorts of people. And your children's friends are often the children of your friends, or people you know. Almost everyone lives within a few miles of each other and all generally enjoy each other's company. Except when they don't, but these things happen. We go to see each other perform in plays; we cringe at each others' letters in the paper; we hear each other speak at town council meetings and meet at the post office and on the trails and in the line for the High Lift and at the doctor's office. We not only know where our children are, but we generally know who they're with, down to the size of their shoes. Heck, down to the smell of their shoes. I'd like to think—and in fact I know—that we look out for each other and each other's children as best we can, through all the joys and of course the sadnesses and even tragedies that occur in any community.

All of this has a surprising effect. Crested Butte is obviously not the most diverse place when compared to America as a whole. At the same time, because everyone who lives there interacts with everyone else far more closely than in a larger city, the range of family friends is more diverse than it might be in an urban or sub-urban or ex-urban bubble where many socialize only with people from their place of work and general age and demographic. My wife and I even know and get along with some people of the other political party, you know, the one where the former vice president shoots his own supporters.

But seriously . . . in an increasingly polarized America, Crested Butte is a place where we live an unusual kind of life. People interact and even socialize with those with whom they might disagree. It is a (mostly) civil place and a civilized place. The children do wear socks, wash fruit (there, I told you), and usually play well together in the sandbox, because that's what their parents do. And that makes it an extraordinarily civilizing place for all of us.

* * *

We don't live in Crested Butte full time any more. And my children are growing older now—Jacob is off to college, and Noah is in middle school. They will look back on their childhood in Crested Butte with love and gratitude. I think of it as one of the greatest gifts my wife and I gave them: magnificent nature at the tangents of their toes and tires, a strong, caring community, and the opportunity to huck sick bird over gigantic rocks.

When our boys do grow older, it may take them a while to figure out how to explain what all of this was like. I imagine each of them at some college bull-session, talking about whether or not you need to have a philosophy of life, the nature of democracy, if science has become a god, what women really want, why men will never figure it out, and so on. As these young people are all testing each other and perhaps becoming friends, they start talking about what it's like where they're from, and my son thinks for a moment and then begins, "Well, where I grew up, the snow banks were so big you could sled on them . . . " and the others laugh and someone says come on, things always look bigger when you're a kid. My son responds, "No, really, they were twenty feet high . . . " and he talks more and soon the rest of them are just listening, listening, wondering, because, honestly, it doesn't sound like many other places at all, anywhere. My son struggles with how to describe it and they continue to listen because his story is so different from their own, strange to them given the way many of them grew up, and most of them have never met anyone from a place like that, who has lived like that, as part of an eccentric village in a pristine alpine valley, ever before in their lives.

Then one of the others will say, "Didn't you ever get bored?"

And that's where I hope my own son just doesn't know what to make of such a statement.

26

Grease

"A man seldom thinks with more earnestness of anything than he does of his dinner." —Samuel Johnson

No matter how hard you ski, there are things you have to do when the skiing is over. One of these things that you must do, on a fairly regular basis, is eat. The harder you ski, the more important eating becomes in the course of any given day. You can only put it off for so long.

When we combine skiing with dining, there are a number of obvious paths to take. There's the high end—Deer Valley's Mariposa or Vail's Left Bank—places where you can get caviar stuck in your mustache at lunch. There's the low end, where the Styrofoam plates won't degrade until the last judgment, and the coffee tastes like it was brewed by soaking bark in dirty snow. And there is the vast middle, the endless array of pedestrian bistros scattered through the ski towns of America, places where the chicken is always a bit overdone, the butter comes on sticky squares of wax-paper, and everyone is trying too hard to convince you to part with more cash than is reasonable for such mediocre fare.

What this list leaves out, what no one seems to want to discuss, are the unforgettable meals on the road after a day of skiing, when your head is spinning with tales of untracked glory and you drive through the darkening landscape toward your next encounter with winter and gravity. One of the unsung pleasures of a ski road trip is eating delicious food you know is bad for you, the kind of rocket fuel that makes gentler souls shudder even to contemplate.

These places aren't ski town restaurants. They sit conveniently on roads between ski areas, outside the orbit of resort prosperity and corporate sponsorship, waiting to fill the craving in your gut for something real, a grease bomb, a heart missile, food that can replace the jillion or so calories you've just burnt on the hill. Some of them are near nothing, others are ten or twenty miles down the road from some uncrowded, unknown, epic hill.

Even the names of these eateries are magical: The Chief, The Shooting Star, The Red Dog Saloon, The Duck Inn (ok, that last one's not so magical). You've probably never heard of them, but they are classics, institutions you can hit with a big appetite and a bad case of hat hair that no one will see because it's okay to eat with your hat on. Their menus are so dietetically incorrect they'd make your mother weep. But facts are facts, and the fact is that serious skiers and snowboarders eat a lot of food that the government and a wide range of independent consumer organizations frequently remind us is dangerous. We eat it in places like this.

Below, to give you a more concrete sense of what I'm talking about, I assess a few delightful dives that deserve wider recognition. I don't offer my list as authoritative, but rather to testify (courageously, I think) to the much-maligned joys of immense burgers, onion rings, and soup of the day.

* * *

THE CHIEF is a classic east coast diner that sits just east of the Taconic Thruway on Route 23 in Martindale, New York. The nearest ski hill is Catamount, one of the larger Berkshire areas, about fifteen miles to the east. I first went to The Chief when I had fled New York City for a day to climb and ski Mt. Everett, a beautiful little mountain in southwestern Massachusetts that is traversed by the Appalachian Trail. I was in a rush, but my companion, Paul "Thunderbolt" Muscat, insisted that we stop at The Chief. In fact, he refused to go skiing without his cup of Big Chief Jo.

Everything about The Chief is authentic, from its gigantic neon Indian head sign to the torn upholstery in the booths. The waitresses call you "dear" and the specials can be scary. Grizzled locals in flannel sit at the counter and speak to each other in the local code, breakfasts are big, cheap, and greasy, and the coffee is strong. I soon realized the brilliance of Paul's maneuver: we could leave the city before it was safe to walk the streets, bolt a hundred miles north, carbo up at dawn at The Chief, drive another hour or two, then hit the trail tanked up and ready to brave February in the frigid air of New England or upstate New York. Then, on the way home, hungry, smelly, wet, and tired, we could snarf the meatloaf special as we melted contentedly into a tattered seat, playing tunes on our booth's very own individualized juke box. I love The Chief.

* * *

THE DUCK INN is on Route 395 in Kettle Falls, Washington, a lumber town about halfway between Spokane and Rossland, that magical destination just across the Canadian border that is home to Red Mountain, funky radical terrain capital of the interior northwest. The day my fiancée Emily and I stopped at The Duck, jet-lagged and exhausted after driving, flying, and driving again for hours, I thought I was having a flashback to a trip I had never taken. The walls, inside and out, were covered with four-foot high, bright yellow paintings of, well, ducks, and behind the counter stood the largest man I have ever seen, stirring a vat that looked like it had been stolen from a production of *Macbeth*. I liked the place immediately. I told the chef I was famished and he recommended the Duck Burger, which turned out to be about the size of my head and included at least two patties, along with part of almost everything else in sight.

At this point Emily was getting used to my taste in road food, but hadn't yet learned how to order in a place like the Duck, i.e., be careful. She refused to heed my advice and asked for the soup of the day, which was turkey. She remembers it as "cubed turkey mixed with celery that had been cooked until void of nutritional value, in liquid that was supposed to be soup, but jiggled. Maybe it was yesterday's casserole barely warmed over. It was like something that my mother would pull out of the back of the fridge after three months and try to pass off on the dog. There were also saltines. I was afraid not to eat it, because the waitress was sitting down at the table next to us . . ."

After I'd completely demolished the superb Duck Burger, the chef struck up a conversation with Em as I visited the men's room. "That little wimp ate all that?!" he said. "Next time he oughta try my Humongous Burger." Before I left, I told him his cuisine hit the spot and he said, "You know our motto? 'Duck inn, waddle out.' Heh, heh."

The Duck Inn is the kind of place where local papers are left out on the table for anyone to read, and for just a few quarters your coffee cup is bottomless. I can't recommend the soup, but the burgers are awesome, good fuel for Roots, the Slides, and the other triple black-diamond terrain at Red Mountain. Duck inn, waddle out.

* * *

The Red Dog Saloon, on Montana State Route 506, is about fifteen miles south of . . . wait a minute. I don't think I can bring myself to tell you about the last, best ski area. Let's just say it has 2,200 feet of drop with uninterrupted fall-lines from the top of the mountain to the bottom, 1,200 acres of skiing which is rated 65% expert, plenty of snow, no electricity or running water . . . and one (1) lift, which used to be the longest, steepest T-bar on the continent, but has now been replaced by an old chair. The biggest day the area has ever had was about three hundred tickets, and if you can get something like six hundred dollars together and give management enough warning, you and your pals can rent the hill for the day (it's only open weekends and holidays). If you want to find this mountain, you will, and if you're a serious skier or rider you won't tell too many people.

The first day I was at The Mountain Whose Name Shall Not Be Spoken, ripping endless lines with a few locals, they all started saying the same thing at about three in the afternoon: "Are you Doggin' it today?" I couldn't figure out why they kept asking each other if they were tired. They didn't look tired. Finally someone saw my puzzled expression and told me, in reverent tones, about the Red Dog, the only watering hole on the twenty-eight mile access road.

The Red Dog is another one of these places that, if you have any sense of what's great about this country, you will love the instant you walk through the door. It sits out in the middle of Montana winter nowhere, and exhales tall tales. There's sawdust on the floor, pool tables, good beer, and all the funky food you can eat. Most of the people who ski the hill on any given day show up after the lifts close, inflate the events of the day, then wander home even happier. Almost everyone is in the lumber or mining industry in some way. They work hard and they play hard, and they were uniformly friendly to me. At one point, after we'd already spilled a fair share of beer, someone walked up to one of the boys and asked him how he was doing. The reply: "I feel like Dave's hair—totally messed up and out of control." Get thee to the Red Dog.

* * *

THE SHOOTING STAR—I've saved the best for last. I can't hide Snow-basin, Utah, which has become well-known as one of the great lift-served powder destinations in this country. It was the venue for the Downhill and Super G events of the 2000 Winter Olympics, and now there is lift-served access to hundreds of acres of wild expert terrain that was only available via foot before. The resort sits above the tiny town of Huntsville, just east of Ogden, and because it's a bit lower than Snowbird and Alta, it gets only 450 inches of snow a year, a veritable desert by Utah standards.

The Shooting Star is in Huntsville, and claims to be the lon-gest continuously operated bar in Utah (open since 1967—just kidding). Again, it's a not a ski area establishment, just the town watering hole, but most of the local hardcores hang out there after a day on the hill. The bar is wood, the jukebox rocks, the beer flows, the pool table is almost flat, and good times rule. The pièce de resistance is the Star Burger. Owner John Posnien describes it this way: 2 PATTIES, 2 SLICES OF CHEDDAR CHEESE, I GRILLED POLISH KNACKWURST (SPLIT), 3 STRIPS OF BACON, PICKLES, LETTUCE, TOMATOES, ONION, AND SECRET SAUCE. John refuses to divulge the recipe, even when bribed. The bacon is optional, but I went for it because I'm brave. This is one of the best burg-ers I've ever eaten in my life. I know that when I grow older I won't be able to eat things like it—assuming any of us lives long enough, we'll all have to resign ourselves to gumming bad food—but for now, I think of the Starburger as the sine qua non of serious post-powder cuisine. It's also good fuel for the Chicken Dance, which local hero Tom Leavitt teaches to unsuspecting guests. But you'll just have to show up at the Star to find out how that goes.

* * *

This short list scratches just the surface of the vast, unappreciated realm of good bad food for serious alpine adventure. No doubt you have your own favorites. I urge you to patronize them, spread the word, and keep your eye out for more of the kind of culinary character that resort corporations tend to discourage, and cannot create. And the next time you're on the road, a spider's web of wet, muddy gear snarled in the back of your vehicle, remember this as you pull into the parking lot of some bistro as slanted as the cabinet of Dr. Caligari: you may be just another famished powder pig, but you are also part of something that matters, something bigger than yourself, a set of excessive cholesterol traditions that existed long before you did and will continue after you expire. Pull up a chair, give in to your growling hunger, order a burger, fries, and a pitcher of beer, then savor the time you get to spend on the great American road.

PHOTO BY DAVID J. ROTHMAN

27

The Off-Season

After the shenanigans of closing day are over and the drunks with sunburns hucking into the slush have gotten their stitches and gone home; and after the final departure of the last tourists and the buses and the traffic; and after the patrol has pulled all the fences and the chairs are swinging empty in the breeze; and after the town has taken a long, well-earned collective sigh, and most of the restaurants have shut down and school has resumed from its late spring break; then, finally, it gets very, very quiet and the off-season, the mud season, wanders up Elk Avenue like a curious dog.

Other places have maritime snowpacks or Columbia snowpacks. And sometimes in the Rockies we get stable snowpacks that let us ski big lines all winter. But for the most part, we wait. We wait and wait and wait until the snowpack turns into a fat, frozen, isothermic slab, and then we climb early in the morning, when it's still frozen, to ski enormous carpets of corn just as it starts to melt. If it holds snow, you can probably ski it by early May. All that matters is that the night before, it gets cold enough, you get up early enough, and it's a sunny day. You climb with your friends, hit the window right, and descend into the warm valley where the grass is starting to turn green and your kid's purple sled, the one you thought he lost, is sticking out of a dirty snow bank.

Last Saturday I woke up late and decided to ski but figured I would have to find something facing north to make it before the corn went sour. Looking for a quick fix, I hiked the ski area and wound up meeting Baxter, Norton, Ed, Brian, and Jan. They had had the same idea. We went to the peak above the highest lifts, and waited . . . and waited . . . and the wind never backed off in the bright, late April sunshine, and the snow never softened at all and we wound up skiing the Headwall in the middle of the afternoon while it was still frozen as hard as a cue ball, and then I went over to John's and had a beer.

But then on Sunday, sometime after six in the morning, Emily and I met our old friend Dan at the trailhead for the Red Lady. Krista was there with a friend, and then Bob showed up with a friend and we all started climbing. Krista was one of the first people we met when we started coming here twenty years ago. Now she's married, works the patrol, has two kids, and still has that same big smile.

From the top of the first pitch we could see other cars pulling in. At first we all thought we might be a bit late, but it didn't warm up quickly and it had stayed cold the day before so the snow held. Soon we saw another party that had started after us going straight up the bowl and I wondered who they might be, as the guy in front looked like a cheetah. When we got to the top we found it was Pat, who teaches English at the public school and who has won the Grand Traverse and the Al Johnson, so that explained that. Then Allen showed up with a friend and we talked about the good times we've had together in B.C. and how he once got stopped at the border for not being able to remember how many days he planned to stay. I'd say there were about twenty of us on the mountain, including a few younger guys we didn't know.

We poked our noses over the cornice and it was ready and one by one we skied, hooting and hollering down thousands of feet of smooth corn. On the way out, connecting patches of snow down to the road, Bob found a fancy purple jacket hanging from a branch and when we all wound up at Camp Four Coffee eating breakfast, Wouter, who had been in the group with Pat, showed up, and since Bob thought it might belong to Wouter's wife, Jill, he left the jacket on Wouter's truck. But it turned out later that it didn't belong to Jill, so Wouter brought it by our house, and Emily made some calls and found out it was actually Krista's. Meanwhile, back at Camp Four Coffee, Wick came by with some friends and told us how they'd just been on Gothic and he said it was good but they'd had to ski before it softened.

Of course there were other things to do and soon we would have to go do them, but for the time being, it was a lazy Sunday. We were drinking Al's excellent coffee in the sun. The rivers weren't yet running and you couldn't garden and the lifts were closed and the bike trails were still closed and most of the restaurants were closed, and town felt busier than it probably did at this time of year thirty years ago, but the skiing sure was good. It was the off-season, the shoulder-season, we were enjoying it together, and it was beautiful.

One of the interesting things about happiness is that, unlike suffering, it tends not to draw attention to itself. That's part of what makes it happiness. And it was at some point as we were sitting there on the deck of Al's little restaurant in the sun that I quietly realized I was happy, as happy as I could possibly imagine being right there and then. We had just skied perfect snow together off the summit of a 12,500' mountain under a cobalt sky; we were healthy and strong; we enjoyed each other's company; and we lived in a beautiful, peaceful town. "Remember this," I could almost hear a voice saying, "Remember it when the going gets tough. Remember how good life can be."

Interlude

The Sermon on the Mount

And Dick let it be known that he would speak about gear that
    afternoon after dryland,
And behold, the multitude of the team and those who wished to
    make the team did assemble.
And Dick laid out his tools, naming each one as he did so,
The files, cards, clamps, scrapers, stones, bevels, drills, glue,
    an iron, many colored waxes, jigs, screwdrivers, templates and
    more, upon a table in the high school science lab.
And the students gazed upon them in wonder.
And Dick took a new pair of Rossignol Strato 102s which had
    never been drilled
And a pair of the newest Salomon bindings, still in the box,
And lo, he placed the skis upon the lab table
And verily I say unto you he placed the Salomon jig upon the skis
And calibrated it for the size of Karl's Nordica Banana boot.
And in the crowded silence he made the measurements
And then drilled carefully into the surface of the ski,
Sending small curls of plastic, metal, and fiberglass into the air.

And he said, "Blessed are those who work hard: for they shall improve.

Blessed are those who support their teammates; for they shall learn the value of friendship.

Blessed are those who have a good attitude; for it is harder than it at first appears to be to enjoy life.

Blessed are the pure in carve; for to carve a turn is the gospel of St. Warren, and ye shall carve, dang nab it,

Planting the pole in the fall line above the gate, rolling the ankle, driving the knee, dropping the hip in, and following through with a lateral projection, or I'm not your coach.

Blessed are the good sports; for they shall be comforted.

Blessed are they who help out; for there is no 'I' in 'Team.'

Rejoice and be exceeding glad; for we are going skiing tomorrow.

Ye are the salt of the earth; and as for salt that has no savour,

Let it not be thrown out, but be cast on slushy courses to harden them,

To be trodden under fast foot of boys and girls at spring ski camps at dawn!

Ye are the light of the world and because I am a teacher

I love that light even when you drive me nuts in the van.

And enter ye in high above the gate: for wide and easy is the line, and the way broad that leadeth to lateness, and many there be which go in thereat:

Because high is the line, and narrow is the way, which leadeth unto podiums and few there be that find it.

Beware of false prophets which come to you in coaches' clothing, telling you to sit back,

But inwardly they are hot-dogging bozo hackers.

Ye shall know them by their turns."

And the students marveled for he spoke not like a scribe,

But like a coach who was exceeding cool and whereas we had

seen him make such fine turns himself.

And lo, there is more to all this than meets the eye, for as Bill
Koch once said, if more people skied, fewer people might
want to kill each other.

Yes, Sontag, you were inaccurate, rather glib in the urban
labyrinth,

Confusing mountains and the love of them with hatred, how
silly,

Just because Leni Reifenstahl attached notions of virtuous
difficulty to alpinism in some of her earlier films before
working for Hitler.

Glamorous and fascinating skiing and the mountains certainly
are,

But the fact that Riefenstahl became a gifted Nazi propagandist

Hardly translates alpinism into inherently fascist behavior,

For high places are in fact majestic, dangerous and beautiful,

And do require courage to climb and to ski, and do inspire awe.

Reifenstahl will have to take responsibility for her own
subsequent behavior,

So let's let go the notion that her alpinism is of a piece with it,

Lest we also totalize our own thinking about such things.

Let fascism be fascism and mountains be mountains.

Furthermore, many skiers fought the fascists, not only our own
10th Mountain on Riva Ridge

But also Austrian Jew Ernie Blake, calling three of the gutsiest
runs at Taos

Oster, Fabian ("Schlabrendorft," his last name, too tough for
tourist tongues), and Stauffenberg, who, executed at 36 when
his bomb failed to kill Hitler, shouted "Long live our sacred
Germany!" as he fell to the floor.

And consider Hannes Schneider, the greatest skier of them all,
probably arrested by the Nazis because he may have jilted Leni

after they co-starred in Fanck's 1931 *Der Weisse Rausch*,
A great ski film with no fascist undertones as far as I can tell, no
    proto-Nazi sentiments or premonitions of Führerworship,
Just a lot of talented people ripping hard,
Which may look fascist from a distance, but only if you're not
    a skier.
Schneider fled to New England and Toni Matt of Inferno fame
    escaped to Mt. Cranmore; Friedl Pfeifer to Sun Valley, and
    many more.
No, it's not just a game, and it's not reducible to politics.
It's something much more than that, this love of mountains.
And there, thirty-five years after the war, in a public high school
    science lab in those gentlest of gentle hills, the Berkshires,
Dick Hurlbut passed on to us what had been passed on to him
And I say unto you that he did it with joy and humor in his heart,
Working to teach us how to think for ourselves.
And I hope he has, over these many years, forgiven me for
    jumping off a bump too near him at the base of Bromley the
    following year, landing on him
And breaking his leg,
Which understandably upset him, although he told me, from a
    cot in the Patrol shack at the base, where I stood, about to cry,
As he was looking out the window at how beautiful a day it was,
That I really couldn't do a damned thing by sticking around,
So I should go back out and ski the rest of the day and have a
    good time.
Yes, verily, let it be said that it was love itself.

28

Sweet

I hadn't brought my skis. It was late May and we were just back in town for the weekend. And it had been a big snow year but I figured some of the bike trails would be open, even if just the low ones. I was looking forward to getting on my bike and prowling around. I could handle a little mud.

As we came over Monarch and down into the Gunnison Valley, we got the first sign that biking wasn't going to happen. Fifteen hundred feet below the base of the lifts, the valley looked like a drowned rat. North-facing hillsides still had enough snow to bury the sage and even the south-facing pitches sported big cornices and long vertical ribbons of deposition where snow had built up in the lee. The river sprawled out over the valley floor and looked more like a lake. Even the weather was shaking its head, a storm moving in with low clouds running from the southwest.

Up in town, there were large piles of dirty snow on the north side of every building and where the plows had stored it. Rotting, long-buried trash was slowly coming to light. At a time of year when people are usually at least trying to rake their lawns, this year they were still assessing the damage. The upper crossbeams of every fence and railing were broken. An external staircase had been ripped right off the side of our house. What a year to move down to the front range, even if most locals who had stayed for off-season had a slightly demented look. "Yeah, a big year," they'd say, "Over four hundred in town." A pause, and then, "I can't believe it's snowing again."

Because it was. Rain and flakes, a mix, but soon enough it began to stick. I didn't bother to take my bike off the car. Then the next day, with snow on the deck, I started scavenging in the garage. I dug up a dusty pair of orange Tecnica alpine race boots and some ancient powder boards, Dynastar Bigs. An old ratty pack, some rusty extendable poles, a hat, bibs with a busted zipper, burly winter slip-on sneakers with big treads.

Emily asked, "You're doing what?" And I said I was just going to climb the area, see what's going on, there was nothing else to do anyways. She shook her head, as she usually does after more than twenty years. I don't mind.

It's been a long time since I've gone backcountry skiing by carrying an entire alpine rig on my back. It reminded me of hiking into Tuckerman Ravine in high school. I started up at the base of the hill where management had plowed out the roads and there were perhaps two inches of wet fresh snow. Still, it was obvious that there was continuous skiing to the base more than six weeks after the lifts had closed. There was no one else around and no tracks.

A thousand feet up and out of view of the base area, there was now four inches of snow and it was beginning to dry out. The road cut above Upper Park was over my head and the snow so dense I began to wonder if it was going to transform into glacial ice before it ever melted. When I reached the top of the Queen, 2,200 feet above the base, there was six inches of new snow and the top several inches were getting fluffy. The sun was peeking in and out of the clouds and temps were in the high twenties. I began to get that feeling, you know the one: I'm going to get lucky. The stars are aligning. I'm holding the right lottery ticket.

My ankles were soaked above the winter sneakers, but I had dry socks in the pack. And that pack was heavy. Even if I had no one to blame but myself, I did feel a bit like a slave of the ancient Egyptians, carrying a block of granite on a tump line up an incline steep enough to choke a donkey. But at the top of the High Lift, 2,700 feet above the parking lot, it was winter. The storm had broken, but streamers of gray cloud were protecting the snow from the full force of the spring sun. The northern wind washing around the back of the exiting storm also kept things cool and I layered up. Pulled the extra socks, lay down my heavy load, changed footgear and locked in. The snowpack underfoot was still deeper than it often is in early March.

As I wrapped around the traverse to the top of the Headwall, luck didn't smile—she grinned, she smirked, she laughed and did a little dance. The wind had blown across the ridge and loaded up the slope until the new snow was about eight inches deep. The surface underneath was frozen so hard I would have needed a chisel to dig a pit and it must have been ten feet deep—the line fell away at more than forty degrees for over seven hundred vertical feet and looked as smooth and soft as the underbelly of a Kashmir goat.

All the effort of lugging alpine gear was worth it for the way it performed. There was enough new snow to fly up over my shoulder and slough a bit on each turn. At the apex of every arc my edges connected for a fraction of a second with the frozen, buried bed and gave a gentle, floating snap to the next move. The sun was in and out, shadows of clouds running across the pitch. A light breeze. Not another creature in sight except for a few small birds. It seemed to last forever, though it couldn't have been much more than ninety seconds. At the bottom I turned and looked back up, snapped a picture on my phone. Then I stood there and drank it all in.

Skiers and snowboarders have a word for this kind of thing. I'm talking about that moment when everything we've ever done or learned meets great snow on a beautiful day in the right place and it all clicks together like the last piece of a beautiful puzzle, or the perfect rhyme, or a first kiss. Luck? Too random. Epiphany? Accurate, but a bit heavy on the religious connotations. Serendipity? Too literary. Timing? Sort of dry. Synchronicity? Too pop-psychological. Grace? Well, in my heart I feel that's true, but it sounds pretentious.

But if you're a rider I expect you'll understand when I use what may be the best word we have, a word that says so much about what life can be when it's as good as it gets. You know this word and you know how and when to use it. You can probably imagine how you would say it, how it should be said, how it can roll off the tongue and lips, slowly, with a sparkle in the eye and a small nod of the head, how much it can convey when it's said right. It's the word that resonated, turn after turn, back down through the mush zone, then the corn zone and into spring. It was the word that returned and returned to me as I walked across the muddy parking lot and drove back into town, savoring every moment, filled with gratitude.

You know what I'm talking about. Go ahead and say it. Say it to yourself even if you're alone, maybe especially if you're alone, to conjure it, to make sure you remember it exists, to keep it alive.

Come on, say it.

Sweet.

29

The Death of a Saint

Colorado has no true glaciers, but it does have scores of permanent snowfields, high folds and nooks and crannies in the lee of the wind that never melt out. The inaccurately categorized but beautiful St. Mary's Glacier, several miles above Idaho Springs, lies in such an eastern lee, under 13,294 foot James Peak. For hundreds of days each year, the wind howls off James and other peaks on the Continental Divide like something out of a storybook. All winter long that wind stunts the trees into fantastic krummholz and sifts spindrift into St. Mary's east-facing, sinuous gully. The snowfield has the added advantage of being within easy striking distance of Denver. A paved road rises to within a half a mile and a few hundred vertical feet of its base at 10,700 feet, and at the trailhead a spacious, maintained, $5 parking lot with port-a-potties greets the faithful. Serious Colorado skiers and snowboarders have always flocked there on sunny weekends in July, August, and September. It's almost a ritual, a little pilgrimage. Riders can easily hike to the top of the snowfield, bag seven hundred vertical feet of skiing on runneled, dirty, slushy ice, enjoy the view, socialize with their kind, and make it back to the car in two hours.

Make that *could*, not *can*. My journal tells me I have skied St. Mary's twenty-seven times in just the last five years, in almost every month. I've skied it many times in August and September for more than twenty years, so when I headed up on September 29, 2012, I was looking forward to the usual good time and survival turns on the bedrock of ice-age infiltration névé.

What I saw shocked me. As I came around the corner of the trail to St. Mary's Lake, where the foot of the snowfield first comes into tantalizing view, there was . . . nothing. Almost nothing. An unskiable remnant of a cornice hung piteously to a few rocks like a dirty pillowcase. Where the snowfield had spilled out for the last twenty (two hundred? ten thousand?) years, even in every September I can remember, now glimmered an apron of barren, naked, almost antiseptic rock that looked like nothing had ever grown on it, which it probably hadn't, as the whole place had been sealed in ice for a very, very long time.

Skiers heading down and out reported there was still some skiable snow above, so I headed up the gully and, sure enough, found the middle section of the snowfield still intact—maybe two hundred feet of skiing, though going fast. Above it, the upper third of the snowfield was also completely gone. Near the top, bent rails and pipes that enterprising jibbers had hauled in lay among the rocks like trucks in a junkyard.

I made my turns, careful to avoid sinkholes opening in what remained of the "snowfield," which looked like less than ten percent by volume of what it had been just a year earlier at about the same time. The day was beautiful, not a cloud in the sky, a gentle breeze, scores of happy, peaceful, friendly people frolicking about, some, like me, even making turns.

2011-2012 was a drought year, but as I snapped a few pictures and headed back to the car, it was hard not to feel something else at work. I had a sense of sorrow, even dread, at the loss of something so wonderful and ancient. The ice of millennia doesn't vanish because of a one-year drought. But why be surprised the change is hitting home? At least we now don't have to go to Greenland to find glaciers and snowfields in retreat. If St. Mary's is any indicator —a dying canary in a very dangerous coal mine—in a few years at most, summer skiing in Colorado is going to be a thing of the past.

And that, of course, is just the beginning of some big changes. I know it's just an anecdote, and I know climate is different from weather, and I know the world hasn't ended when there were massive climate fluctuations in the past. I also don't favor apocalyptic thinking. But if it goes, I'm going to miss St. Mary's, and its sudden vanishing suggests to me it's reasonable to ask, "Why?"

ST. MARY'S GLACIER, LATE AUGUST, 2011. PHOTO BY DAVID J. ROTHMAN.

ST. MARY'S GLACIER, LATE SEPTEMBER, 2012. PHOTO BY DAVID J. ROTHMAN.

30

A Few Lists for Telemark Skiers

We Americans love lists. They make us feel organized, as if we were in control. And there's nothing wrong with that. As long as you remember that you aren't. When it comes to skiing, most lists have to do with things like packing for expeditions, checking snow safety, flowcharts for the technical execution of a carved turn, and so on. In the interest of expanding the spiritual vocabulary of the sport, I thought it might be useful to have a few more expansive lists that get at who we are when we are telemarking. The following lists may not be practical, but may help you to realize you are not alone.

Top 10 Responses to People In High Alpine Parking Lots in June Who, When They See You Walking in Telemark Boots and Carrying a Pack with Skis and Poles, Ask "Are You Guys Going Skiing?"

You are a telemark skier. You like to ski. Sometimes you even go skiing in the summer, because you can walk in those funny shoes, so it doesn't bother you to stroll for a bit to the snow. At the same time, you will take a high alpine road as a point of departure if you can. After all, it's there. When you leave in the early morning, there's usually no one around. But when you return, the tourists have arrived, squinting into cameras, confused. The kids are throwing snowballs. You are sweaty, smiling, carrying a pack with skis, holding poles, wearing ski boots, preparing to pop a frosty one. They look at you and ask you the same astonishing question, every time: "Are you guys going skiing?!"

I know, I know. You're torn between civility and sarcasm. Cut this page out and carry it with you—it may prove useful in a crisis.

10. No, we just went for a hike and found all this stuff up there and figured we'd pick it up. Would you like to come back with us for the bones?

9. No, we're going bowling.

8. Well, not exactly. We just use the skis to get to the croquet course.

7. No. (Mountain Man answer. Just keep walking.)

6. Yes. (More civil Mountain Man answer. Smile, keep walking.)

5. No, we already went skiing. Now we're going to drink beer.

4. Take me to your leader.

3. Yeah . . . can we have a ride?

2. Uh . . . what?

1. Yes, we were skiing, and it was great. Corn like a carpet. See that line over there? Those are our turns. You ought to try it sometime.

Top 10 Lies Telemark Skiers Like to Tell

Telemark skiers generally have a lot of integrity. They're earthy, they're friendly, they're generous, they're tolerant. But they're also human, all too human. And sometimes, perhaps not entirely intentionally, they say things that, while not exactly untrue, may not be exactly true. They might be merely truthy. You know what I'm talking about.

10. You should have been here last year . . .

9. Well, when I used to ski with Kasha . . . .

8. Oh, it was all rain crust and side hills.

7. You should have been here last week . . .

6. Well, when I used to ski with Heather . . .

5. I think leather boots are just more, you know, natural.

4. You should have been here yesterday . . .

3. Well, when I used to climb with Jimmy . . .

2. I've been here before.

1. This snowpack looks ok to me. What do you think?

Top 10 Reasons to Use Duct Tape

Money is expensive. Skiing requires money. Therefore, skiing is expensive. But there are ways around that. Duct tape is one of the ways. I don't entirely trust people who lack duct tape on their garments. Indeed, I have seen cars, or parts of cars, held together with duct tape. This is one of the reasons I like telemark skiers. They understand this. It's like a secret language. The code of the tape.

10. It pisses off your mom/girlfriend/wife.

9. It impresses your dad/boyfriend/husband.

8. Whoever is wearing the greatest square footage is the one most likely to take the lightning strike.

7. Totally waterproof.

6. Stronger than sutures. Faster, too.

5. Lasts longer than student-loan debt.

4. Odorless.

3. Powerfully conveys proletarian sympathies.

2. Looks even more cool when dirty.

1. It works.

Top 10 Reasons Why You Should Not Be the One to Try to Teach Your Boy/Girlfriend How to Make a Telemark Turn

Many of us have tried to do this. If you haven't . . . trust me, leave it to Heather Paul, Dickie Hall, Ross Matlock and other pros. They'll do a better job and you're a lot less likely to wind up sleeping by yourself. Because, for some reason, teaching your significant other how to make a ski turn is apparently as difficult and humiliating for him or her as being in one of those dreams where you're back at your high school graduation, but this time you're naked. It is not appreciated. Do not do it.

10. You will get called names.

9. She will cry.

8. He will sulk.

7. You will feel guilty.

6. Your friends will shake their heads and say "Are you a moron?"

5. Sleeping on the floor is uncomfortable.

4. Sleeping outside is even more uncomfortable.

3. Sleeping at your friend's house creates social debts.

2. Do you have a teaching degree? I didn't think so.

1. Do you really want to be one of those people yelling, "Turn! Turn! Turn!" at the top of your lungs under the chairlift, while some tentative mate does terrified snowplow turns on ice and then tanks it and begins weeping/swearing in public? Yeah, you're more cool than that. Of course you are. Just think about it.

Top 10 Reasons Telemark Skiing is Better Than Sex

10. It lasts longer.

9. The worst thing you can catch is a cold.

8. It's messy, but not that messy.

7. There's no stigma about doing it in large groups.

6. Or with people of the same sex.

5. Or with your dog.

4. After you're done it's socially acceptable to jump up and down and pump your fist in the air, yelling, "That was so awesome!"

3. Mountains never say, "Aren't you going to warm me up first?"

2. Mountains never say, "Look, I'm trying, I just can't find it, ok?"

1. In the end, you're less likely to get hurt.

Top 10 Ways to Tell Someone is a
Telemarker When Off the Snow

Skiing is not a sport; it's a way of life. Telemark skiing is a
particular manifestation of that life. It has its own secret
handshake, its own vocabulary, its own rituals and so it would
qualify in most anthropological handbooks as a culture.
After extensive fieldwork among the natives, while taking
care not to disturb their natural habitat, I have identified the
top ten characteristics of members of this secretive cult.

10.   Most do not pray in the direction of Mecca, but many of the
      men have beards, often with small pieces of granola stuck
      in them.

9.   And that's not genuflecting, it's a turn.

8.   They favor old torn clothing (see number 6).

7.   If you yell "Slide!" they kick off their shoes and start making
      swimming motions. Try this in a Salt Lake City grocery store—
      it's hilarious.

6.   There is frequently duct tape on their old torn clothing. And
      holding their glasses together. And on their cars (see numbers
      8 and 5).

5.   Every pair of ski pants they own has scuffs at the knees, unless
      patched with duct tape (see number 6).

4.   Minimal body fat combined with a sauntering lope.

3.   The women rarely wear makeup or fancy jewelry. Boob jobs?
      Doubtful (interferes with solid pole plants). Occasional discrete
      tattoo or delicate piercing. And they are often disturbingly

beautiful. And, guys, a lot of them could also rip your arm off.

2.   Far off look in eyes. They have seen paradise.

1.   You secretly wish you could ditch your cubicle and become one of them, just to experience what it's like to smile like that again and again for the rest of your days.

Now you know, or perhaps you know more than you did, or, if you don't, you know how you might learn it. Even though Lou Dawson has argued that if you free your heels, your edges will follow, still, telemark skiing remains a beautiful thing. The natives are friendly. Feel free to join me in my research.

31

The Cap

A few years ago I moved from Crested Butte, where I'd been living for about fifteen years, down to a small city of the plain that sprawls up against the mountains. It was time, for a number of reasons. We wanted different opportunities for our children; our parents were aging and found it a challenge to come to nine thousand feet above sea level, especially in the winter, making it hard for them to see their grandkids; career opportunities beckoned; we ski hard, but eight months of shoveling gets a bit annoying; it might be fun to grow a tomato; and so on. And when it came to the skiing, I was antsy for new terrain on the lifts and in the backcountry, despite how much I love what's so easily accessible from my old haunts.

We settled into our new home, where the mountains rise only in the west. Then, one day in October, I decided it was time to go get the picture taken for my new (and far less expensive) ski pass at the local hill, which is fifty minutes from my door, up a long, two-lane canyon into the high country. As I stood there in the little office the resort maintains down in town waiting for the plastic to laminate, I looked through the sweatshirts and key chains and other paraphernalia bearing the resort's logo.

They call the mountain a resort, but one of the reasons I like it is that it isn't. There are no detachable quads, let alone gondolas or trams; there is no real estate for sale at the base; in fact, there is only one main base area. The shuttle across the potholed and muddy parking lot to the carefully segregated learning lifts and the Nordic center is a yellow school bus that lost any semblance of shocks decades ago. The skiing sprawls along a ridge and there are dozens of trails but only about sixteen hundred feet of vertical. No one is threatening to tear down the funky bar with big wooden beams at the base and replace it with a "bistro" that tries to serve better food, does a bad job, but charges a lot. There is no Jumbotron. The outdoor speakers on the lodge are a tiny, tinny Wal-Mart affair. Everywhere you look people are keeping it real in jeans and parkas with the names of sports teams. Many of the hardcores are tele-markers, and they rip. There are long, steep, gladed tree lines that appear on no trail map, the kind you learn about by talking with the guys pouring the beer. The race program is large and well run and has a short, dedicated Poma. Almost everyone here on any given day lives within a two-hour drive and all will drive home after the lifts close. No, this is not a ski resort; it's a ski area, the kind that reminds me of the places I grew up skiing, such as Snow Basin.

Snow Basin was in a pocket that received some of the heaviest snowfall in the Massachusetts Berkshires, which could be quite a lot in most of those years. To be a child hanging out there was to live inside a charm. It had 550 feet of vertical drop and three T-bars—which seemed plenty for us, given the way the terrain twisted and turned and pitched. And yes, there were glades that were not on the trail map. The couple who had founded it, Stan and Ruth Brown, knew skiing and knew how to lay out a hill. Ruth had been a national caliber racer in the 1930s, and Stan was her coach. So of course they had to make a joke out of that and call one of the runs "Ruthie's," something I never got until I took a year off from college to race and moved to Aspen.

By the time I was in high school in the 1970s and we were running GS from the top to the bottom, Snow Basin was a second home to me and my friends. I even used to spend weekend nights sleeping at the home of the Ski School Director, Ken Cyr, who lived across the street. When I was a senior, there was a party there one Saturday night with an old guy named Bo. I don't know why, but he was playing a washtub bass and someone was sucking the big toe of his left foot. Everyone was yelling "Suck Bo's toes!" and laughing so hard they could barely talk. I remember thinking that adults could be very strange. I think I get it now. They had help.

That same year we convinced the management to let us build a huge kicker with a snowcat right at the bottom of the hill, big enough to throw triple-daffies and 720s, practically landing in the parking lot. Those same adults would smile and shake their heads and get a certain look in their eye. A full-length GS was over a minute from the top to the bottom and we trained on all-natural snow. Everyone knew everyone else. The lodge didn't have a cement floor, just dirt covered with a three-inch layer of smooth stones. The food was delicious, especially the sticky buns, and although Stan had died in the 1960s, Ruthie, her hair gone white, was still working behind various counters when she must have been well into her seventies.

The area closed decades ago now and the trails have grown in, but many of the people who lived nearby and trained there went on to be serious skiers, racing in college and even still today on the master's circuit, such as my old friend Rick Slabinski, the Slab, a very quick skier I could never quite catch.

So I stood there in the shop of my new ski area at the foot of the Rockies and picked up a jet black ball cap with white stitching. It was made out of heavy fabric and bore the name of the ski area on the front, also etched in white, above the bill. Its second line read C. 1963, and the third said MOUNTAIN RESORT. On the inside, the brim sported a tag that said AHEAD EXTREME, and another that boasted EXTREME FIT. And another that said MADE IN CHINA. Well, ok, what isn't anymore? Burly Velcro strap. I modeled it in a mirror.

The kid running the desk told me my pass was ready and I brought the cap to him and said I would buy it, too. I ran the string through the plastic and put the pass around my neck so I wouldn't lose it on the way home, and put on the cap. At that moment, without expecting it, I could feel my little world tilt on its axis. I hadn't bought a season's pass at a new ski area in fifteen years. In fact, I'd only ever had passes at six other hills in forty years: Mt. Tom and Snow Basin, both in Massachusetts and both now out of business, when I was a kid; Pat's Peak, in Henniker, New Hampshire, where my college team trained; one year at Aspen Highlands, before it was part of the Aspen Ski Corp.; Snowbird for three years when I was in grad school and skied enough powder to choke an elephant; and then Crested Butte.

If you're a skier—really a skier—shifting your allegiance from one hill to another is a big deal. It means not only new terrain and new people, but a different culture: different topography, different slang and nicknames, a different schedule, a different way to think about the hill, about the day, about where to go when, about what's good to eat in the lodge, about the weather.

In my first year as an Eldora skier, we had good snow. Jacob had a breakthrough as a J3 racer with their team, which runs like a Swiss watch. Noah, who was then six, skied his first black diamond, a long rolling run with a good pitch called "Muleshoe" that was slicker than snot the day he decided to try it. I came to understand why people at this hill laugh when they talk about receiving a foot of wind the night before. I found a killer full-length glade on the front of the mountain, the entrance in plain view from the lift, though only the hard-cores seem to know about it. I realized that an eighteen-meter turn radius was too long for the steep tight trees at this hill and so I bought another ski along the lines of fourteen or fifteen meters max, so I could stick those beautiful tight sneaky lines in Brian's Glade with a bit more panache. I met some very cool people. I learned which aspects soften up first in the spring sun. I had the ritual beer or two in the base lodge bar with friends after skiing, before everyone headed down the hill. I learned that the breakfast burrito is the way to go when my son is on the hill for early morning training, freezing his little gonads to his leg. I found the backcountry gate, I figured out how to link a sweet line through the tight, steep Placer Glade (come on guys—cut some trees).

We are like icebergs, only the tips showing, or hippos grazing a river bottom, only their eyes visible. Our invisible stories, some of them happier than others, are mostly below the water line. So I forged a few good new memories this year, and so did my family, especially our sons, though you couldn't tell it by looking at us. Here in the Rockies, the sun is bright. I almost always wear that black cap when heading outside, and if someone asks me what the word on the front stands for, I say, "That's my ski area. Great place. Most underrated lift-served hill in the state . . . Let me tell you about it. Do you ski?"

32

On Going to Bed

Although many animals have specific times of day, month or year when they procreate, most are indifferent about location as long as it meets utilitarian and fairly broad environmental parameters. Even higher order and relatively intelligent vertebrates, e.g., dogs, generally do not, unless rigorously trained and sharply ordered to desist, stand down for environmental context, but basically hump at will. Once they're ready to proceed, the world is, so to speak, their oyster. No tomcat, goldfish, frog, microbe, hummingbird, or goat in rut ever turned to his or her partner and said: "Not here— it's just too icky." In fact some of the smaller ones are what made the place icky in the first place. For them, nature is everywhere and sex just *happens*.

So why not us? Because, come on, admit it . . . when we are really honest with ourselves—stare-in-the-mirror, acknowledge-the-grief, contemplate-our-flaws honest—shouldn't we admit that lovemaking and the natural world go together about as well as air-planes and tornadoes, or birds and windows, road kill and mustard?

My musings are not merely theoretical. I believe in testing

abstractions against the pulse of experience. Most of the times I've tried to get it on in the great outdoors have wound up resembling a Marx Brothers movie more than, say, *Swan Lake*. They weren't even deliciously lustful and nasty—just incredibly uncomfortable.

Once, in college, my sweetheart and I decided to make love under a spreading apple tree in a field. We were young and coupled vigorously and successfully. She spread her long skirt, sat astride me, I penetrated her deliciously, and we were rather proud at how we were enjoying ourselves undetected, even though cars whizzed by on a country road not a quarter of a mile away. Cows munched bucolically. Then, as we began to grind towards a juicy, sweaty, shared climax, I realized that an insect was trying to crawl into my rectum, which unfortunately meant that I had to move my hand.

"Put it back in!" she said, "Put it back . . . .!"

"Ouch!" I said. She gave me such a sad look.

In the end, it all worked out. We were both smiling. And all was well until a few hours later, when I realized that either a tic or a spider had defended itself from our invasion by taking a huge bite of my ass, injecting poison that swelled up to the size of a red, angry silver dollar and hurt like hell for a week, making it almost impossible to sit.

Several years later I was living in a foreign country teaching English. Not only did I look different from everyone there, the government of this particular country made it its business to have a lot of control over everything. I mean *everything*. My relationship at the time was on the rocks and a lovely young woman from yet another country offered to ease my pain. We made off into the woods one cloudy, ink-black night and had a wonderful time rolling around on pine needles gently kissing each other, etc. Until we heard some rustling here . . . and there . . . and saw some movement here and there . . . and realized we were being watched, at a respectful distance, by what appeared to be a small battalion of locals committed to upholding the Decency of the People. No doubt if that happened today we would have awakened in the morning to emails featuring our glistening buttocks all over YouTube.

Another time several years after that, when my wife and I were courting, we snuck off her parents' boat, found a mossy bank in the deserted woods of an island in the Gulf of Maine, ripped off our clothes, and proceeded to have about half the blood sucked out of our bodies by a swarm of mosquitoes even more ecstatic than we were, because they probably hadn't seen so much raw flesh in their entire short lives. A few years later, living in the Colorado Rockies, now married, we decided to try it on a summit we'd just conquered. Again, we succeeded, naked and coupling like goats well above twelve thousand feet, but not before my beloved's lips began to turn blue. I should add that it's hard, under such circumstances, to tell the difference between cries of joy and exclamations about a rock that is pressing on a kidney.

In the end, the reason sex feels so incredibly good—perhaps better for humans than for most other animals if our idiotic behavior is any indication—is that our offspring are dependent for so long. The delicious road to orgasm short-circuits the wakeful part of the cortex that knows what will happen if the woman gets pregnant: eighteen years of servitude. My children are the joy of my life, but that's my story and I'm sticking to it. Every cell in the body starts screaming: "Don't think! Stop paying attention! Go, dog, go!" This siren's voice can easily overwhelm every other kind of common sense, so why not trample the still, small voice that calls out for a little physical comfort? As in: "Don't we need a pillow?" or "Gee, it's raining." But here, in the calm and thoughtful space of discursive practice, we can and should be somewhat more discriminating. We are free. We can choose. Sort of.

Haven't thousands of generations worked hard to invent things like satin, in-floor heating, and hot water on demand? Most natural

environments just aren't conducive to the distracting practical com-
plexities of penetration, including, say the option of cleaning up
afterwards. In addition to those described above, where I and one
or another beloved were assaulted by venomous insects, unwanted
observers and harsh elements, there have been other encounters
where I learned how sand and friction don't mix, how distracting
prowling animals can be, and so on. It's all fun and games until
you need stitches and a tetanus shot.

There's a funny video clip that made its rounds on the web a
few years ago of a handsome couple somewhere in the Alps who
belay into space from an immense, overhanging outcrop of rock.
In their climbing harnesses, twirling in the breeze with terra firma
nowhere in sight, they proceed to have fairly acrobatic sex. One of
the interesting things about the footage, however, is how many shots
it obviously took. I just wish I could hear some of the outtakes . . .

"OK, uh, can you swing over this, oops, no, not there, more to
the—ouch, hey, look out!"

"Sorry, do you want me to—wait, you're too low, I—you know,
I really need to pee—"

"Yeah, ok, uh, can you guys pull us up for a few minutes? The—
oh, sorry, was that your stomach?"

"No, I'm fine, really, but I can't feel my right leg."

In the end, it hardly seems worth it, unless you're getting paid.

So I conclude with the humble proposition that, as beautiful as
the outdoors can ever be, it is preferable to encounter it clothed
and to keep it a wall or two distant from any passionate embrace.
I spend as much time as I can in the outdoors, and a lot of it on
mountains, but as romantic as it may seem, screwing on a rock or a
beach or in a field or a forest is often uncomfortable and sometimes
dangerous. Tigers, spiders, porcupines, rhinoceroses, sparrows
and dolphins are better suited for that kind of thing than we are,
because they have claws, armor, wings, flippers and small brains.

Perhaps we're spoiled, but perhaps we should leave it to them. We should let the wilderness reside in our hearts and encounter it mostly clothed rather than getting down in it like monkeys. After all, monkeys have opposable thumbs on their feet and more hair. It's a kind of *nostalgie-de-la-boue* hubris to think we can swing like that. In fact, it may be that civilization itself was born the very day the two creatures who became the first man and woman looked at each other, sighed and said, "You know—I think this would probably go better in the cave."

My love, her breasts are indeed like clusters of grapes, and her stature like unto a palm tree. The smell of her nose is like apples, her teeth like a flock of sheep which have come up from the washing and her temples like a piece of a pomegranate. But, gentle reader, let us remember in our ardor, the articulate ardor that burns so brightly within us, that those are similes, and we are but human.

And for humans, bed is best.

33

Why I Telemark

Somehow I knew about it even when I was a kid growing up in New England. My friends and I would try to figure it out on skinny skis on the local sled hills, clambering around on track gear and falling down again and again. But we didn't take it seriously and could never quite make it work. We didn't worry about it. We wanted to go fast, very fast. We craved big power, locked-heel rocket fuel that could snap bamboo. Other subtleties were just a little too subtle.

After my sophomore year in college, I took a year off to ski race and saw the Rockies for the first time, living in Aspen. In February of 1980 we went to a race in Crested Butte, which in those days was still a renegade outpost where people went to hide out, a bit like Butch Cassidy and the Sundance Kid's Hole in the Wall. I still remember riding up the old, slow Paradise double and watching some moss-faced maniac drop out of the forty-five-degree trees in the Tower 11 Chute and cross under the fall line on skis about as wide as fishing poles. Peruvian crash helmet, leather boots, knee bent low, skiing a line as technical as anything anybody was attempting on alpine gear. Then, a few years later, now living in Salt Lake

City, I went out for a day in Emigration Canyon with Wyn Cooper, a fellow graduate student in English at the University, and after a day of flailing around in breakable crust, humiliated and soaked to the bone . . . I was hooked.

Why? Love is complicated. I can imagine all sorts of details, but at the heart of it is always a mythology. I love the wild bunch who look like they've eaten too much acid and haven't bought new ski pants since 1987. I love the long, lean women who know how to saunter so gracefully in boots. I love the fact that I'll never be as good a telly skier as an alpine skier. I love sitting around in a cabin in Ophir with dear friends talking about the Drunken Frenchman, educational administration, and Mr. Toad's Wild Ride. I love the fact that Dicky Hall can convince 152 telly skiers to try to make a turn all holding on to each other. I love trying to find the sweet spot of grace as opposed to the heavy-metal axis of swat (although I love that too). I love flexing the ball of my foot.

I love the new gear. I love watching my old friend Lance ski, like a ball of mercury flowing down hill. I love the way his sister Lise calls me "Pussy Dog," laughs, belches like a jester, then rips the West Drain. I love the way my wife Emily found joy in skiing through telemarking, a joy she could never quite find on alpine skis. Soon she was skiing Colorado fourteeners and big burly avalanche tubes on pins. I love walking the mountain instead of stomping it, which is a good thing, considering how much less cartilage I have than I used to (from all that stupid stomping). I love tweaking the corporate ski consumer culture. I love the way the movement connects back directly to the ancient roots of the sport. I love the secret handshake. I love Kasha Rigby (well, who doesn't?). I even love the way Lou Dawson says "Telemark skiing? Hah! Free your heels . . . and your edges will follow," laughs that way he has, then takes off uphill like a cheetah.

I still alpine as much as I telly. It's not a religion. But there is something indefinable about free heel skiing that draws me back to it again and again. It's a little more difficult, a little more graceful, a little more free, a little more quiet, a little more friendly, a little more subtle, a little more pure. Pure what, I'm not sure. But more than that, a day of telemark skiing connects me with the mountains and with my companions in a way that may not be better, but is definitely different from a day spent locking the heel, which can come to feel a bit like drag racing.

In the end it comes back to that myth, which is, like all myths, a story about being in relationship with the creation, or at least the recreation. As for what is being recreated in such turns . . . it probably can't be described. But when I find that sweet, sweet spot at the heart of a free-heel turn, whether telemark or Cristiana, I also find that, at least for those brief moments, such balance isn't a situation, it's a place. And in that place, that relationship, I can't be balanced unless the earth is somehow balanced too, right there against the ball of my foot.

I ski—and especially I telemark—to be in that place. Come on, planet: let's dance.

34

Where Does it End?

Where do the mountains end? When does the skiing stop? Where
is the edge of the cause that led to these effects?

For some, it's at the close of their vacation, when they hand
in the rental gear. For others, it happens around Easter, when the
drive no longer seems worth it. Next come those who hang it up
only after closing day, going into summer with a raccoon-eyes tan.
Then there are those of us for whom the silence of the bullwheels
is just a blip on the screen, who keep hiking into the mountains,
chasing the snow up the valleys. When I first moved to Colorado
I skied more than thirty months in a row, ferreting out dirty September snowfields on high northern exposures as old-timers just
shook their heads and laughed.

But this is only one way of thinking about where the mountains
and the skiing end. How could we ski without imagining skiing?
Look at the best gate skiers and it's always the same—they're not
looking at their feet. The eyes are up, several turns ahead, the turn
in process already almost history, the next one the only one that
really matters. We see their bodies working, but if we look more

closely we can also see their minds.

So, if you are imagining the next turn, whether one second, one month, or one year away, isn't that part of your life in the mountains? What about those conversations with friends, planning that hut trip? What goes through your head when you are putting your gear away for the summer (if you do . . .) or when you are reading about skiing (as you are now); what about all the things you've learned because of skiing, about geology, and geography, and weather, and people, and who you have become as a result?

Twenty years ago, I was living in Salt Lake. One day, standing in line on the Snowbird plaza, I met Neil and Jan, and we hit it off, skied hard all day, became friends for life. Neil is a Kiwi who comes to Snowbird every year. At well over sixty, he still hucks big rocks and eats lunch out of his pocket on powder days. He's also the inventor of Fly-by-Wire, the ultimate amusement park ride. Jan makes hand-painted silk scarves. He's recently become the executive director of a consortium of summer adventure youth camps on the Hood River Gorge in Oregon. Back then, every year he'd hold a gathering of friends at Alta. When Jan learned I play the piano, he told me that Bruce, an old Chamonix roommate, was coming out and since Bruce was also a pianist, Jan would rent a piano that week and we could both play. Which we did. Then Bruce, who is now a magistrate in Denver and an excellent pianist, and I went skiing on a huge powder day and Bruce told me there was this beautiful girl he'd met a few times who was the daughter of friends of the parents of his former partner in some real estate venture, and he thought they might have a condo this week every year and lo and behold, twenty minutes later we skied up to the Gad 2 Chair, and there was Emily. Although she was extraordinarily pretty, it was a powder day, so off we went. First things first.

The next night I went to a party because Mack, who I met racing NCAA's back east, was in town, and there was Emily again, because she had grown up with other people who'd also raced with Mack and they were around that week too. And then it turned out that Emily and I were living half a block apart in Greenwich Village, and as you can imagine at that point there was no way I was going to pass up trying to get a date with a woman that beautiful, who it turned out was a dancer and could make me look like a duck just by getting off a couch. And I was scheduled to administer the oral exam for her undergraduate degree at NYU, where I was a grad student, though by the time that came around, I had to recuse myself.

Over the years we've all stayed friends. Bruce took me up my first fourteener, Torrey's, still one of the best corn runs of my life—a northwest spillway dropping over 3,500 vertical feet with the final turn spraying corn like Prosecco onto the hood of the car. I think that's the time I met Pete, a gifted photographer who used to patrol at A-Basin. And Bruce introduced me to Steve, a friend of his from the University of Denver law school, who now runs a mutual fund in Boulder, and he's the one who organizes our yearly trips to British Columbia, where we've skied some of the best huts in North America: Golden Alpine Holidays, Fairy Meadows, Selkirk Mountain Experience, mountains rippling away forever like waves. On the day I introduced Bruce and Steve to backcountry powder on Teton Pass, we wound up skiing with Doug Coombs and spent over an hour digging pits—a great day. That was the week in 1997 he got booted from Jackson Hole. Doug was a gifted guy and it's important to remember that he didn't die "skiing." He died while in rescue mode, trying to help someone else. Whatever bad luck he may have encountered that day had only to do with his attempts to help a friend.

And Emily and I are married and she is the mother of our children, Jacob and Noah. She had never been backcountry skiing when we met. But the weekend before I wrote this essay, as the sun was rising, we scrambled three thousand feet up the southeast pitch of Gothic, a 12,600-foot laccolith just to the northwest of Crested Butte. At dawn we skirted a mating pair of grouse, his feathers up in peacock display as he pursued her through the brush, and soon after we strolled across the summit ridge to the top of a couloir with a southwest aspect that I'd been eyeing for a dozen years. It drops straight off the peak and holds a solid forty-degree pitch for more than two thousand vertical feet before backing off into meadows and glades that lead back to the road. We waited, just the two of us, for ninety minutes on the summit and then skied that entire line on corn with the consistency of Mr. Bubble. And Emily ripped it (on pins).

In return, she has made me into a devoted balletomane. If there is reincarnation, I want to come back as a gifted dancer (who skis); that would make me a bit like Crawford, who danced for BalletWest and is now a hotshot orthopedic surgeon in Boston, last I heard. But that's another story, one of thousands, and anything I could ever write about all of them can only be a grain of sand on the beach. What I can say is that I wouldn't know many of my dearest friends, or even my wife and my own children, without mountains, mountain towns and skiing. I wouldn't know myself. And that wouldn't change if I never made another turn in my life.

For many of the people I love, mountains and skiing are not scenery; they are a cause, in the sense that they make things happen. In my life, so many of those things have been good ones that it isn't a stretch to call it all a blessing. Eventually that's what it comes to: gratitude.

So where do the mountains end? When do the turns stop?

Maybe they don't. Maybe the nature of the deepest causes is that they are not what we think of as causes at all. And how can one explain the conundrum: the lever that seems to move the world is the world itself? Maybe the secret of life is that there are no mere effects, because all of them are also causes.

And the ways that truth works itself out in your own life? That, my friends, is worth contemplating.

EMILY AT CONEY'S, CRESTED BUTTE BACKCOUNTRY, 2013.
PHOTO BY DAVID J. ROTHMAN.

35

The Dude in the Parking Lot

Last May, leaving A-Basin after one final day for the year on the lifts, I saw a strange sight. I had crossed under the highway and clanked up the stairs into the overflow lot, and as I was walking to my car I saw some random guy standing there, looking up at the ski hill, tears streaming down his face. I stopped for a minute, unsure of what to do. But he looked at me, smiled, and then without saying a word, got into his car and drove off with the stereo pumping The Rolling Stones. *I tell you love, sister, it's just a kiss away, kiss away, kiss away.* He pulled out onto Route 6 and punched it towards Loveland Pass, mud flying everywhere.

I had to laugh. It hadn't been a great day. There was a cloud cover that wouldn't break, so while the snowpack was good, it only softened up at the end of the day and even then not on all aspects. There was some dry, creamy snow left high in the reaches of Montezuma, but even most of that side skied like frozen cookie dough and the visibility was lousy everywhere. At one point, still searching for something better, I hiked up from the top of the Lenawee lift to the East Wall and jumped into Notch One, only to realize that what had looked smooth from below was as hard as a lawyer's heart and similarly studded with small pieces of granite. Wearing a pack and sporting a free heel I did have to wonder why I was risking a five hundred-foot slide for turns that felt a bit like riding a jackhammer.

By three o'clock, despite the anemic light, the beach was in full cry—barbecues, costumes, Frisbees, jumping dogs, lawn chairs, spontaneous boom-box dance parties, beer flowing like subprime mortgages in the old days, kids having snowball fights—and the front had finally softened a bit. The bumps were big and almost forgiving on Palli and Exhibition. In the last few years the Rockies have been getting multiple major spring dust storms, so the snow was dirty—but it was sliding well enough.

I was about ready to quit by that point. I'd had my left hip resurfaced for arthritis just nine months before, had only skied on the lifts about twenty times for the season, and the hard snow was making me squirm.

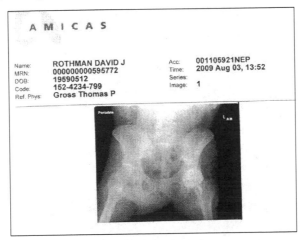

It would be an understatement to say the surgery, performed by the amazing Dr. Gross of Columbia, South Carolina, had been a success. By the time I was forty-five, my hip looked like the oldest cue ball in a biker bar; I walked with a limp and knew my days on skis were numbered—a fine reward for a roaring life filled with gates and hucking. A number of friends in Crested Butte told me Gross had changed their lives, so when the insurance came through, I made the decision. What did I have to lose?

A resurfacing is not a replacement. It involves no pins, screws, plates, adhesives or moving parts, and the patient loses almost no bone. Instead of cutting off the head of the femur and replacing it with a mechanical joint, in a resurfacing the surgeon caps the femoral head with a hollow, cobalt-titanium hemisphere that's held in place only by a peg driven into the top of the femur. There's a small, similarly shaped receptacle on the acetabulum. The two pieces of metal separate the arthritic combatants, and voilà—with a little luck, the problem is solved and the patient can go back to full activity. In my case, I woke up in the recovery room and the pain in my back that had harassed me for a decade was going . . . going . . . gone. It was gone like a payday bonus, gone like a mouse into a cat, gone like a hardball heading for the bleachers, gone like bipartisanship in the Senate. Six months later it hadn't returned, my recovery was suitable material for a triumphant textbook, and I was free to ski again, which I started to do, gently. I hadn't put in a full, hard day on the lifts in years because it would leave me crippled the next morning, but that spring I skied day after day, a little more each time. I went to Snowbird, skied deep snow, and even made the climb, gingerly, up to the ridge above Gad II and skied Scotty's with my older son, Jacob, then fifteen.

As I was heading for the parking lot that afternoon at the Basin, I passed by the demo tents. I'd been meaning to try some rockered skis, but the year before it had hardly seemed worth it, as I'd been thinking I might soon have to stop skiing forever. I was drawn to the Ski Logik tent by the cool graphics and the shapes and got into a chat with a guy named Darrell. Before I knew it, my skis were stashed in a corner and I was riding up Exhibition with a pair of Howitzers dangling from my toes.

The Howitzer is designed as an all-mountain board. That year, it came in only one length, 186 cm. It sports a moderate rocker and has a 22-meter turn radius with a 137/110/131 profile. It looked a little long to me, but no, said Darrell, sizing me up and smiling like the Cheshire Cat, no, man, you're gonna love 'em, they're going to rip.

I got off the lift, put my hands through the straps while still moving, bent into a turn, and the ski turned so fast I wound up going backwards. I only ski reverse switch, so this was a surprise. I spun around laughing, headed for the big corn bumps of Exhibition and almost immediately felt something I hadn't felt in a while, something that conjured memories of being six years old and charging down the same hometown hill again and again, flying and happy. I had a new hip, nothing hurt, and although I was keeping the boards on the snow more than I once did, there I was, charging VW-sized slush bumps at A-Basin, the rock and roll drifting up lazily from the jam band at the base. The skis were so dynamic and stable I felt they were practically egging me on. "Come on, Dave, why are you holding back? The lifts close in forty minutes . . . We're burning daylight. Come on, man, *punch it!*"

The turns kept getting better and better as I figured out the Howitzer's sweet spot, which isn't hard to find, because it's huge. If this ski were a food, it would be a fruit smoothie laced with adrenaline. I threw four quick laps, tightening the lines through the rollers each time, caught the last chair and wound up with a feeling I thought had left my life forever, that glow that seems to come from every muscle when the body and spirit feel in tune with the hill, the snow, the gear, even the air. I was filled with completely inappropriate and unjustified feelings of friendship and love for all living things.

When I handed back the skis, the Patrol was already on sweep. I talked with the guys in the tent for a while, then headed for home. That's when I came up into the parking lot and saw that goofy guy standing in the mud, in the flat light, looking up at the mountain and crying.

Pretty funny. The snow had been mediocre, the light weak, and it never warmed up. But, on reflection, I think I get it now: all that really matters is being there. That's all that matters and you need to try to get as much of it as you can, because the chance may never come again. And who knows? It hadn't been such a great day, but maybe it was one of the best days that guy had seen in years. Maybe that's what he was thinking.

I can imagine that.

After all, he looked a lot like me.

THE AUTHOR TOPS OUT ON THE GUNBARREL COULOIR ON MT. OWEN, NEAR CRESTED BUTTE, COLORADO. PHOTO BY JEFF SCOTT.